Comic Potential

Born in London in 1939, Alan Ayckbourn spent most of his childhood in Sussex and was educated at Haileybury. Leaving there one Friday at the age of seventeen, he went into the theatre the following Monday and has been working in it ever since as, variously, a stage manager, sound technician, scene painter, prop-maker, actor, writer and director. These last two talents he developed thanks to his mentor, Stephen Joseph, whom he first met in 1958 upon joining his newly formed Studio Theatre Company in Scarborough. A BBC Radio Drama Producer from 1965 to 1970, upon the early death of Stephen Joseph he returned to Scarborough to become the company's Artistic Director. He holds the post to this day, though the theatre is now named after its founder. He is the author of over fifty plays, most of which received their first performance at this Yorkshire theatre, where he spends the greater part of the year directing other people's work. More than half of his plays have subsequently been produced in the West End, at the Royal National Theatre or at the RSC. They have been translated into over thirty languages, are seen on stage and television throughout the world, and have received many national and international awards. Alan Ayckbourn was appointed a CBE in 1987 and in 1997 became the first playwright to be knighted since Terence Rattigan.

ALAN AYCKBOURN

Comic Potential

faber and faber
LONDON·NEW YORK

First published in 1999
by Faber and Faber Limited
3 Queen Square London WC1N 3AU
Published in the United States by Faber and Faber Inc.
a division of Farrar, Straus and Giroux Inc., New York

Typeset by Faber and Faber Ltd
Printed in England by Mackays of Chatham plc, Chatham, Kent

All rights reserved

© Alan Ayckbourn, 1999

Alan Ayckbourn is hereby identified as author of this
work in accordance with Section 77 of the Copyright,
Designs and Patents Act 1988

All rights whatsoever in this play are strictly reserved and application for
permission to perform them must be made in advance, prior to any such
proposed use, to Casarotto Ramsay & Associates Ltd., National House,
60–66 Wardour Street, London W1V 4ND

*This book is sold subject to the condition that it shall not, by way of
trade or otherwise, be lent, resold, hired out or otherwise circulated
without the publisher's prior consent in any form of binding or cover
other than that in which it is published and without a similar condition
including this condition being imposed on the subsequent purchaser*

A CIP record for this book
is available from the British Library

ISBN 0-571-19787-6

2 4 6 8 10 9 7 5 3

Characters

Adam Trainsmith, a young writer, early 20s
Chandler (Chance) Tate, an American director in his late
50s
Lester Trainsmith, Adam's American uncle, 80s
Hotel Desk Clerk
Hotel Waiter 1
LM05623, an actor android (playing the Doctor) (seemingly 40s)
LM05623, an actor android (playing the Farmer)
(seemingly 40s)
Man in dress shop
Turkey, a pimp
LJM 54823, a male actor android (playing the Son)
(seemingly 20s)
Marmion, American, speaker for Lester Trainsmith
Hotel Waiter 2
Technician
JCF 31333 (Jacie Triplethree), an android actress (seemingly mid 20s)
Trudi Floote, a technician, 30s
Girl in dress shop
Prim Spring, a programmer, 30s
Carla Pepperbloom, the Company's Regional Director,
age unknown.
CW 77502, an actress android (playing the Mother)
(seemingly 40s)
CW 77502, an actress android (playing the Farmer's
Wife) (seemingly 40s)
Dress Shop Assistant
A Prostitute

Act One
Scene One: A TV studio. One morning.
Scene Two: The same. Later that day.
Scene Three: The same. A few days later.

Act Two
Scene One: The studio. The same day.
Scene Two: The Grand Hotel Foyer. That evening.
Scene Three: The studio. The same evening.
*Scene Four: The Grand Hotel Boutique. The same
evening.*
Scene Five: The studio. The same evening.
Scene Six: The Hotel Restaurant. The same evening.
Scene Seven: The studio. The same evening.
Scene Eight: The Hotel Bedroom. The same evening.
Scene Nine: The Hotel Mombassa. Later that night.
Scene Ten: The studio. The next morning.

*Time: The foreseeable future when everything has
changed except human nature.*

Comic Potential was first performed at the Stephen Joseph Theatre, Scarborough, on 4 June 1998 with the following cast:

Adam Trainsmith Nicholas Haverson
Chandler Tate Keith Bartlett
Lester Trainsmith, Hotel Desk Clerk,
   Hotel Waiter 1 John Branwell
The Doctor, The Farmer, Man in dress shop,
   Turkey James Hornsby
The Son, Marmion, Hotel Waiter 2,
   Technician Bill Champion
Jacie Triplethree Janie Dee
Trudi Floote, Girl in dress shop Pippa Hinchley
Prim Spring Jennifer Luckcraft
Carla Pepperbloom Jacqueline King
The Mother, The Farmer's Wife, Dress Shop
   Assistant, A Prostitute Helen Pearson

Director Alan Ayckbourn
Designer Roger Glossop
Lighting Kath Geraghty
Costume Designer Christine Wall
Music John Pattison

A new production was first performed at the Yvonne Arnaud Theatre, Guildford, by arrangement with Michael Codron in association with Lee Dean, on 28 September 1999, and subsequently presented by Michael Codron in association with Lee Dean at the Lyric Theatre, London, on 13 October 1999 with the following cast:

Adam Trainsmith Matthew Cottle
Chandler Tate David Soul
Lester Trainsmith, Hotel Desk Clerk,
   Hotel Waiter 1 John Branwell
The Doctor, The Farmer, Man in dress shop,
   Turkey James Hornsby
The Son, Marmion, Hotel Waiter 2,
   Technician Bill Champion
Jacie Triplethree Janie Dee
Trudi Floote Becky Hindley
Prim Spring Eleanor Tremain
Carla Pepperbloom Jacqueline King
The Mother, The Farmer's Wife, Dress Shop
   Assistant, A Prostitute Helen Pearson
Girl in dress shop Suzannah Hirst

Director Alan Ayckbourn
Designer Roger Glossop
Lighting Kath Geraghty
Costume Designer Christine Wall
Music John Pattison

Act One

SCENE ONE

The TV studio.

The lights are bright on a hospital bed. The Young Man lies in some pain. His Mother stands crying. The Doctor is with her. In the corner lurks a Nurse holding a clipboard.

Barely discernible in the gloom, watching this, are the director, Chandler, the programmer, Prim, and the technician, Trudi.

Doctor (*gravely*) ... I assure you, we've done everything we can, Mrs Crayshaw. But, as I say, the bone is just too badly shattered ...

Mother (*weeping*) No, no ...

Young Man (*bravely*) Don't cry, Mum, for God's sake don't start crying ...

Mother It's so cruel ... cruel ...

Doctor Surgically speaking, we can do a lot these days but we're still a long way short of miracles, I'm afraid.

Mother Why my son? Why Alex?

Young Man Doctor, will I have to lose the foot?

Mother Alex, don't ...

Young Man I have to know, Mum. It's my future we're talking about here! If I'm never going to walk on that field again and kick another goal, I want to know about it, don't you understand that?

Mother We won't give up, darling. We'll fight it. We must fight it ...

1

Doctor (*a trifle impatiently*) Look, Mrs Crayshaw, you're only making things more difficult for your son. (*clicking his fingers*) Nurse!

The Nurse hands him the clipboard she is holding. The Doctor passes it to the Mother.

There! You don't have to be an expert. Just look at these X-rays, woman. They speak for themselves. There's massive damage to the foot. I'm going to have to operate immediately. I'm going to remove the temporary pluster cust and umputate just above the unkle . . .

The Nurse laughs.

Prim (*angrily, at her console*) Oh, no . . .

Chandler HOLD IT! Hold it! What is it saying? Prim, what the hell is it saying now? Umputate his *uncle*? Is that what I heard?

Prim I'm sorry, Chance . . . It's not my fault . . .

Chandler Umputate his *uncle*? (*indicating the Nurse*) And what is that one laughing at? Does anybody know?

Prim (*slightly hysterical*) I don't know.

Chandler (*to Trudi*) Do you understand all this? You're supposed to be the engineer. Enlighten me, please.

Trudi It sounds like random AU subrogation to me . . .

Chandler In English, *s'il vous plaît* . . .

Prim It's replacing its As with Us, that's all . . .

Chandler Is it?

Prim Just occasionally. It's a vowel problem . . .

Chandler That's all I need. A leading actor with vowel problems. Its As with its Us?

Prim That's all it is . . .

Chandler Tremendous. We'd better keep it away from the fax machine then, hadn't we?

Trudi (*checking the Doctor*) The signal's clear at this end . . .

Prim It's not the signal, it's internal somewhere. We have to do something, Chance, it's getting steadily worse . . .

Chandler (*to Trudi*) So why doesn't she fix it?

Trudi It's internal. I'm a technician not a cyber surgeon . . .

Chandler (*threatening the motionless Doctor*) Useless tin hunks of –

Prim Don't hit it . . .

Chandler (*checking the blow, returning his spleen towards the Nurse*) And what's the matter with this nurse?

Prim Nothing.

Chandler It was laughing its head off.

Trudi Yes, I noticed that.

Prim Well, that I can't explain. Certainly nothing to do with me. Right. Shall we try again? I've taken us back two lines.

Chandler Come on then! Come on! We are two hours behind, people!

Prim Thirty-seven minutes behind.

Chandler Let's roll it, then, monsters. And, Prim, can you give me more tears from the mother? The woman is supposed to be heartbroken. Her little pride and joy's about to lose his foot and she sounds like someone with mild hay fever . . .

3

Prim Check. (*She makes an adjustment, muttering.*) I just didn't want to make it gross, that's all.

Chandler Gross? Since when did we worry about gross? That's what they want out there. The grossest story ever told. Sixteen million viewers can't be –

Prim Fourteen.

Chandler Fourteen? I thought we were sixteen. Since when are we fourteen?

Prim Since last week.

Chandler Why am I the last to hear? I am the director. Why am I not told this?

Prim Because you never read anything I put in front of you.

Trudi What's a fax machine?

Chandler A fax machine. You never heard of a fax machine . . .?

Trudi New one on me.

Chandler She's a technician. She's never heard of a fax machine.

Prim You have to make allowances, Trudi. Chance is technically still in the twentieth century . . .

Chandler What kind of a technician's never heard of a fax machine . . .?

Prim Nobody's ever heard of a fax machine, they went out twenty years ago.

Chandler So what? The age of steam is also dead but I've still heard of steam engines. Despite genetically engineered, self-levelling grass-seed, I've still heard of a lawn mower . . .

4

Prim All right! All right! Can we get on, please? We are now thirty-nine minutes behind.

Chandler All right. Arses in gear. And . . . action! (*immediately*) Hold it! Who says I don't read things?

Prim I put it on your desk. You tear it up. You set fire to it.

Chandler I only burn irrelevancies . . .

Prim You don't even know Mrs Pepperbloom is coming today, I bet . . .

Chandler Carla Pepperbloom?

Prim Yes.

Chandler The Black Death is coming here?

Prim Any minute.

Chandler Shit! What does she want?

Prim She didn't say.

Chandler Shit! And she didn't say what for?

Prim No.

Chandler Shit! Do you think it's about the drop to fourteen million?

Prim I don't know. Ask her.

Chandler I don't ask her. I don't even speak to the woman. It's about the fourteen million, it has to be . . .

Trudi If we don't finish this episode, it'll be eight million . . .

Chandler Who cares? Show them an old episode, they'll never know. When's that going to bother our viewers? They're all subnormal, anyway . . .

5

Prim Would you not say that, please? That is offensive.

Chandler Low IQ TV. Especially produced for people who can't figure out how to turn on the set . . .

Trudi That is now very offensive . . .

Chandler Good.

Trudi Has he been drinking?

Prim Probably.

Chandler All right, people. Let's go to work! Action!

The lights brighten on the playing area and the action resumes.

Doctor Just look at these X-rays, woman. They speak for themselves. There's massive damage to the foot. I'm going to have to operate immediately. I'm going to remove the temporary plaster cast and amputate just above the ankle . . .

Chandler By Jove, he's got it!

Mother (*weeping softly*) I can't bear it, I just can't bear it . . .

Chandler She's a pain in the arse, this woman. Are we planning to kill her off soon?

Prim Certainly not. She's our most popular character . . .

Chandler That figures. They always are, the ones I loathe.

Doctor I just don't know what more to say, Mrs Crayshaw . . .

Chandler Don't say anything, Doc. Quit while you're ahead . . .

Mother (*still weeping*) Oh, dear God.

Chandler Hell, this is depressing. Give the mother more tears, more tears, please.

Prim I've already given her –

Chandler More tears! Who's directing this?

Prim All right! All right! (*She stabs at the console rather savagely.*)

The Mother lets out a keening wail.

Chandler Better!

Prim We'll get letters again.

Chandler Burn 'em!

Young Man (*yelling above the din*) Don't turn away, Mother, you can't hide your tears from me . . .

Trudi This is ridiculous . . .

Doctor (*inaudibly, over the Mother*) The point is, Mrs Crayshaw, there have been amazing advances in prosthetic surgery in recent years . . .

Chandler What are you complaining about? At least we can't hear the doctor.

Doctor (*ploughing on regardless*) . . . these days a hand, a foot, a whole arm can be replaced and to all intents and purposes you can forget about it entirely. Even the wearer themselves. People play squash, tennis, even go mountaineering without any ill effects whatsoever . . .

Chandler That damn nurse is laughing again, what's the matter with it . . .?

Prim I've said I don't know. I'm toning the Mother down, Chance, I can't face any more of those letters.

She does so. Under the next, Carla enters with Adam.

*They watch until they are noticed. Adam is fascinated.
The Mother quietens down as Prim recalibrates her.*

Doctor   Needless to say, a lot of it is due to the immense
strides we've made in the field of android development in
the past few decades. Take the hand for instance. An
android's hand, of course, is not that different from one's
own. They feel the same to the touch and they are
designed with equivalent humanoid movement, with all
the flexibility you'd expect from a human hand. Finger
muscles, wrist action – virtually indistinguishable from
the real thing. Only of course about fifty times stronger,
let's not forget that. (*He laughs.*) Looked at in the long
term, and on the positive side, your son's new foot, once
it's up and running, will actually outlive the rest of him by
several decades . . .

Chandler   (*during this*) This man could bore for Britain,
do you know that?

Prim   (*indicating the visitors*) Chance . . .

Chandler   What? (*seeing them, rather over-genially*) Mrs
Pepperbloom, by all that's glorious, good morning to you!

Carla   (*icily*) Good morning, Chandler. Please, don't let us
interrupt . . .

Chandler   Not at all, any interruption is most welcome.
Prim, dear, could you turn the volume down a little for
us? Monitor on headset.

Prim   (*reluctantly*) If I must.

*Prim and Trudi don headsets. The hospital scene runs
silently under the next, during which the Mother leaves.*

Carla   Good morning, Prim.

Prim   Good morning, Mrs Pepperbloom.

Carla You're still as passionately involved as ever in programme-making I see, Chandler.

Chandler Art needs room, Carla. It requires space. It doesn't want a director crowding it. He needs to stand back.

Carla Don't stand too far back, will you, you might fall off altogether.

Chandler Oh, my word! Perish the thought!

Carla This is Adam, whom I mentioned in my memo.

Chandler (*ignoring him*) Yes, of course. How nice.

Adam How do you do, sir. It's a very great honour to –

Chandler A new young executive accountant, no doubt. Here to advise us humble artists on programme-making. Adam who?

Adam I just wanted to say, sir, that I –

Carla As I mentioned, this is Adam Trainsmith . . .

Chandler Trainsmith. Trainsmith?

Carla Lester's nephew.

Chandler (*digesting this*) You're Lester Trainsmith's nephew?

Adam Yes, sir.

Chandler What the hell is he doing here, Carla?

Carla I explained it all in my memorax, Chandler –

Adam I wanted to come, sir. I asked to come.

Chandler Here?

Adam Yes.

Chandler Why?

Adam Because of you. I wanted to meet you. As I say, sir, you're my greatest living idol. After Hal Roach and Preston Sturges, I think you're just the finest –

Chandler What is he doing here? Is this about the figures? Is that what it is?

Carla Figures?

Chandler The audience figures. Is that why you're here?

Adam (*bewildered*) I'm sorry?

Chandler Has he come to take over, or what? (*rising, angrily*) Come on, sit down, kid, take my chair, what the hell. They're bringing them straight out of the playpen, but then any fool can direct these days.

Carla Chandler!

Prim Could you keep it down a little, please!

Adam Sorry.

Prim I know they're only actoids but they still need to concentrate.

Carla Chandler, Adam is here because he's a great admirer of your work, apparently. God knows why . . .

Chandler An admirer?

Adam Yes.

Chandler (*indicating the set*) You're a fan of *Hospital Hearts*?

Adam No. Well, in a way. No, it's your early work. Your movies, Mr Tate. I've got them all. I study every inch. I try to learn from them. Your timing, your choice of angles, your editing. Your wonderful sense of comic –

Chandler All right! Yes. Terrific. So you dig up the dead, do you? What are you? Some kind of gravedigger? Get this adolescent necromancer out of here. I've got a programme to make. (*He turns away abruptly.*)

Carla I'm sorry, Adam, I did warn you he was filled with old-world charm.

Adam (*confused*) What did I say?

Trudi You reminded him.

Adam Of what?

Trudi The past.

Carla (*running her fingers through Adam's hair*) He's such an innocent.

    Adam looks uncomfortable.

Isn't he too lovely?

Trudi Beautiful.

Carla Oh yes, of course, I was forgetting. Hardly your type. Well, I must dash, Adam, darling. I will be back. I leave you to savour the delights of Chandler Tate. I won't be long. I promised your uncle on pain of death I'd take care of you . . .

Adam I'll be fine. You don't have to –

Carla (*kissing him on the mouth*) Goodbye, sweet boy. I shall be back to take you to dinner. *Au revoir*, everyone.

Trudi Bye.

Carla Oh, Chandler.

    Chandler turns to her reluctantly.

I see the viewing figures have slumped rather dramatically. I know we're only minor league here, but twelve million is touching the bottom of the barrel, dear.

Chandler Here it comes . . .

Carla We'll have to do something about it, won't we?
You can't drop any lower. And if we move you sideways
any more you'll be out of the building.

Chandler Turn the volume up a little please, Prim. I can't
hear properly. There's somebody talking over the programme. Totally unprofessional behaviour.

Prim (*as she does so*) Just coming up to credits . . .

   Music under.

Carla (*almost inaudible*) See you later. (*She goes.*)

Doctor (*genially*) Listen, old chap, I've been a surgeon
here for longer than I care to remember. And, I'm
delighted to say, I've never lost a patient yet. And I'm
damned if you're going to spoil that record, all right?
Let's get that straight, shall we? This is a perfectly
straightforward, run-of-the-mill aparation.

   The Nurse laughs. The others react.

Prim Oh, no . . .! Hell! Hell! Hell!

Chandler (*with her*) I don't believe it! I simply don't
believe it!

Trudi (*with them*) Oh no, not again!

Adam (*a beat later*) What did he say?

Prim Shall we take it again?

Chandler No. Remix the music over the top. Drown him
out. Who cares?

Prim We can't. It was important plot.

Chandler What plot? Drown him out!

12

Prim All right.

Adam What did he say just then?

Chandler Did you see the nurse? It was at it again. Laughing.

Prim I know, I know.

Trudi We weren't on the nurse. We were tight on the doctor.

Adam Did he say aparation? I thought he said aparation?

Chandler Next break we have, I want that doctor booked in for cyber surgery. I don't care about the waiting list. I am not working with it in that condition again. If they won't mend it I'm writing the doctor out . . .

Prim I'll try my best. We do have very low priority, Chance. We're only –

Chandler I don't care. Make it so, helmsman. (*wheeling on Adam*) I'm sorry. You wanted to see me?

Adam Yes. I was hoping to talk to you –

Chandler Treat the place as your own. I will be back. You'll find movies, you'll find books, you'll find everything you want.

Adam Yes, but I was rather hoping to –

Chandler Just ask Prim. Prim is a treasure. She'll show you. (*as he goes*) Trudi!

Trudi Yes, Chance?

Chandler Get that nurse on the bench, do you hear me?

Trudi Yes, Chance.

Chandler sweeps out.

A silence.

Adam I was rather hoping . . . Where's he . . .?

Trudi A little liquid refreshment. Thirsty work, directing.

Adam Oh, I see.

Trudi Don't follow him. He always drinks alone. (*to Prim*) I'll put the doctor on diagnostic again.

Prim It's something internal. It has to be.

Trudi I know. Show willing, anyway.

Prim Random internal. That's the worst. It was AO that time. I adjusted for AU and he starts AO.

Trudi It'll be something in the speech processor.

Adam (*who has been staring closely at the figures*) These are amazing.

Trudi Never seen one close up?

Adam No. Not actually in the – flesh as it were . . . Amazing.

Trudi Not all that amazing, unfortunately. (*referring to the Doctor, to Prim*) Are we on manual?

Prim (*switching from the console*) Going to manual.

Trudi (*to the Doctor, brusquely*) Come on, this way. Follow me, doc.

Trudi goes off. The Doctor follows her obediently.

Adam (*ineffectually, as they go*) Can I help in any . . .?

He stands, rather lost. Prim continues tidying her console, ignoring him.

Well. (*regarding the Nurse*) I wonder what she found so funny.

Prim How long have you been with Carla?

Adam Sorry?

Prim How long have you been with her?

Adam Oh. Only a few hours. She picked me up yesterday at the airport, and we drove straight here this morning.

Prim Oh, I see. You're not together then?

Adam No. (*laughing*) No. Certainly not. (*considering the prospect*) God. No.

Prim I'm sorry. I think we all assumed you were . . . her latest . . . You know. Sorry. She seemed to be claiming ownership, anyway.

Adam Yes. It's a little embarrassing. She was doing that in the car this morning. The chauffeur had to pull the blind.

Prim She has quite a reputation.

Adam She does?

Prim The Pepperbloom babes. She gets older, they get younger. Sorry if it sounds bitchy but that's a fact.

Adam (*laughing*) I'll just have to fight her off.

Prim Just be careful how you say no to her, that's all. She doesn't like it.

Trudi returns.

Trudi I've left it on diagnostic. (*to the Nurse*) Sit, nursie!

Obediently, the Nurse sits.

Prim So Lester Trainsmith's your uncle?

Adam That's right.

Prim That must make you considerably rich.

Adam No. That makes my uncle considerably rich. I come from the poor side of the family. Well, poor compared with Uncle Lester.

Trudi (*plugging the Nurse in to the console*) Like everyone else. So what are you doing here?

Adam I'm a writer.

Prim Oh . . .

Trudi (*unimpressed*) Uh-huh.

Adam I – simply admire Chandler Tate. I always have. I think he's just the most fantastic director.

Trudi Really?

Adam Don't you?

Prim Well, he may have been once but . . .

Adam Some of his films are classics.

Trudi Are they?

Adam Have you never seen any?

Trudi No.

Adam Anyone who loves movies should see them as part of their education.

Trudi We're in television.

Adam What's the difference?

Trudi He wants to know what's the difference. Look around this place. That's the difference. This isn't even television. This is local television.

Prim Not even local, it's branch-line TV.

Adam It seems fine to me. All this gear. The actoids . . .

Trudi This gear is fifty years old. You need a diploma in archaeology to work it.

Prim I don't know why you think you're here, Adam, but this is where you come to end your career, not launch it.

Adam I don't see it that way.

Trudi Lunch, then?

Prim You want to join us?

Adam I think I ought to wait here for Chandler – he said he'd be back.

Prim Wouldn't count on it. P.M. is not his strongest time of day.

Adam I'd better wait. Don't want to offend him any more.

Prim Suit yourself. Look around. Oh, and if you like his movies they're probably all in his drawer there. You know how to work the viewer?

Adam Sure.

Prim Incidentally, don't call him Chandler. He hates it. He prefers Chance.

Adam Oh, right. As in lucky chance?

Trudi As in positively his last.

They start to leave.

Adam Oh, what about . . .? (*He indicates the Nurse.*)

Trudi It'll be OK. If it starts whistling, just pull its plug out.

Adam (*doubtfully*) Right.

Prim and Trudi go out.

Prim (*as they go*) Where are we eating today?

Trudi Surprise me. Surprise me.

Adam, on his own, looks around. He is intrigued by the Nurse. He walks round her a couple of times, studying her.

Adam Now, why did you laugh just now?

He opens the drawer that Prim has indicated.
He takes out a file box of small video disks.
He studies their titles in turn.

(*As he does so, approvingly.*) Good . . . oh, great . . . wonderful . . . yes . . . (*suddenly*) Hey, I cannot believe this. He's got *this*? He's got this!

Adam excitedly inserts the video disk into a slot on the desk.
The sound of a silent movie piano. A large (invisible to us) screen lights up above his head.

Oh, yes!!! (*searching the desk*) Fast forward? Fast forward?

The disk screeches as it fast forwards.
Adam finds the section he wants. He watches intently. He laughs at the action. He laughs again.

This is just so brilliant. (*He laughs.*)

Behind him, quite suddenly, the Nurse laughs.

(*jumping in alarm*) Oh, my God. You're alive? What am I going –? You're live! Are you supposed to be live?

Nurse I'm active, yes.

Adam Well, are you supposed to be? Should I be unplugging you or something? I was supposed to unplug you if you whistled.

Nurse Then I promise not to whistle. (*looking at the screen*) Who is this?

Adam This is one of the greatest silent comedians the world has ever known. His name was Buster Keaton. Have you heard of him?

Nurse No.

Adam He ran his own studios for a time, way back in the early 1920s. Silent comedy. You know? Comedy without words.

Nurse No words?

Adam Keaton broke new ground because – Excuse me. Are we conversing?

Nurse Yes, I think so. I'm listening. You're talking.

Adam Yes. Is that –? I mean, you are a – an – aren't you?

Nurse An actoid, yes.

Adam And you talk?

Nurse Oh, yes. An actoid needs to talk. Unless they're Buster Keaton. (*She smiles.*)

Adam smiles back.

Adam This is ridiculous.

Nurse Why?

Adam I don't know. I just didn't expect to be having a conversation. Do you always talk to people like this?

Nurse No. Normally people don't converse. It's quicker to direct link through the computer.

Adam Then why now? Why me?

Nurse Because you're talking to me.

Adam And do you have a name? I mean . . .

Nurse Oh, yes. My name is currently Bridget Bonny. Nurse Bridget Bonny.

Adam No, that's the name of your character, surely?

Nurse That's right. (*slightly Yorkshire*) I'm twenty-four years old and I was born in Halifax, Yorkshire but at a very early age my parents moved south to –

Adam But what's your real name?

Nurse (*a little puzzled*) My real name?

Adam Your real name. You must have a real name?

Nurse Oh, yes, I see. The name I was made with. It is JC – F31 – triple 3.

Adam Jacie? Pretty. May I call you Jacie?

Jacie If you wish.

Adam I'm Adam.

Jacie Yes, I heard.

Adam Tell me, Jacie. I'm interested. What made you laugh, during the filming? At the end there?

Jacie I don't know.

Adam Did you find it funny?

Jacie Yes. I'm afraid I have a fault.

Adam Not necessarily. Just because you laugh doesn't mean you have a fault.

Jacie It just happened. I had no control.

Adam No, that's natural. We see something funny, we laugh. Involuntarily, sometimes. We can't help ourselves.

Jacie I think I have a fault.

Adam You found Keaton funny, too?

Jacie Oh, yes. In a different way. That little look he gave.

Adam The look? Oh, you mean the take?

Jacie Take?

Adam The double take. You know about double takes?

Jacie No.

Adam It's a well-known comic device – the double take – or in Keaton's case the quarter take. The demi semi minuscule take. But at the other end of the scale you have someone like – let's see – James Finlayson – Finlayson's a good example. He was famous from the Laurel and Hardy movies. Do you know the –? No? Well, Finlayson would do takes where he literally took off and left the ground. Bold massive takes. Like this.

He demonstrates badly. Jacie looks puzzled.

Really funny. When he did them. Do you need to stay plugged in?

Jacie Yes.

Adam OK, stay sitting down, I'll teach you. Right. Let's see. Imagine you're reading a book, yes?

Jacie I'm reading a book.

Adam You hear me come into the room . . . You know it's me, so you don't look up at once. What you don't know is that I am covered in mud. I have fallen in a puddle outside the house and I am covered in black slimy mud from head to toe. You look up casually, you see me, register my presence but your book is so interesting you go quickly back to it. You do that . . .

Jacie does so.

Now, as you look at your book again, the image of me suddenly registers on your brain. You realize what you've seen. You look at me again. Quickly, sharply this time. Amazed.

Jacie does so.

All right. Let's do the whole thing. You're reading your book. Here I come. Covered in mud.

Adam clumps rather heavily into the room. Jacie glances at him, then back at her book.

Jacie Hallo, dear, is it raining?

She does the rest of the take.

Adam (*impressed*) Good! Excellent. Your first double take.

Jacie Was it all right for me to put in the line?

Adam Er . . . yes. Yes, that was fine. It wasn't strictly necessary but it was fine. Good. We'll make a comedian of you yet.

They smile at each other. Adam executes a rather clumsy comic trip.

Whoops!

Jacie frowns.

Next week, the custard pie.

Jacie The custard pie? Is that funny?

Adam In the right hands. It's a – it's basically just a pie. Full of custard – or usually cream. Flat on a plate. And – when someone annoys you – or gets up your nose – you know – (*miming*) – you take the pie and you squash it in their face and you twist it – like that – so it –

Jacie – goes up their nose –

Adam You got it.

Jacie That's funny?

Adam Er – not to talk about, no. It's a visual gag.

Jacie Custard pie . . . (*She copies his mime.*) Yes, that could be funny.

> *She smiles at him and laughs. He smiles and laughs, too. They stare at each other. Adam looks away, rather embarrassed suddenly.*
> *The lights fade.*

SCENE TWO

The same. Later that day.
> *The team are all assembled and in the midst of more recording.*
> *The Doctor is in full flow. Jacie, as the Nurse, hovers in attendance. The Young Man, still in bed, listens weakly. Chandler, slightly the worse for drink, sprawls in his chair, watching disinterested. Prim and Trudi are beavering away, doing all the work. Adam watches intently like a child in a toy shop.*

Doctor . . . but I'm afraid there's also some bad news, Alex . . .

Young Man Doctor? Is it my foot? Is it . . .?

Doctor No, as I say, the foot's a runaway success. We'll have you chasing around again in a matter of weeks. No, I'm afraid it's something rather more serious than that. It's your mother, Alex. I'm afraid she's – well, to put it absolutely bluntly, I'm afraid she's dead.

Chandler Hooray!

Young Man Dead?

Prim They're not going to like this, Chance, she was the most popular character . . .

Doctor In the car park. An umbulance on a mercy mission. It was very quick.

Prim Oh, sod it! (*to the others*) Sorry.

Doctor She felt nothing. I am so very sorry.

Chandler We'll put some music in here. Big strings. (*He whistles tunelessly.*)

Trudi We'll be down to five million by the weekend.

Doctor Now then. Let's have a look at those stitches, shall we? Nurse! Pull back his bedclothes, will you?

Jacie (*moving to do this*) Yes, doctor.

Chandler Come in close on the boy, Trudi.

Trudi Yeah, I got it.

Chandler Tears! Prim, I want more tears from that arsehole . . .

Prim (*irritably*) All right, all right.

The Young Man sobs helplessly. Jacie draws back the bedclothes. She glances down at the Young Man. She executes a double take. It favours the excesses of Finlayson rather than the niceties of Keaton.

Chandler (*as this happens*) . . . that's good . . . that's better . . . I like it – (*seeing Jacie, yelling*) WHAT THE HELL IS THAT NURSE DOING? Hold it, hold it! Stop everything. (*losing it*) Prim! Have you no control over these things at all? You're supposed to be a programmer, what are you playing at?

Prim It wasn't me! That wasn't me!

Adam Listen, I think that was –

Chandler The nurse doing takes like Zero Mostel on speed, a programmer who can't do her job —

Adam Listen, I think that was –

Chandler You shut up! No wonder the place is running down. I'm surrounded by incompetence every place I turn.

Prim (*angrily*) Don't you blame me, I'm not the one who changes a successful storyline just for the hell of it –

Chandler That's called –

Prim – cuts out characters just because they're popular –

Chandler – that is called artistic choice, woman. Not that you'd know anything about that –

Prim That's what's known as pig-headed, bone-stupid crassness . . .

Chandler You're a fuck useless artisan, what do you know?

Prim (*indicating the actoids*) And don't swear in front of them, please! I'll be editing swearwords out of every episode on top of everything else . . .

Chandler Oh, namby pamby wah! wah! wah!

Prim Yes, well, somebody has to do it, Chance. If it wasn't for people like Trudi and me, you'd have been in the street years ago.

Chandler Oh, ballsuckers. I was making major movies when you were . . .

Prim You come in drunk, you shout, you swear, you expect everything to happen just by magic and you never even bother to say thank you!

Chandler All right! Thanks for nothing. How about that?

Prim You drunken – pig. I don't have to work with you. I have – qualifications. Which is more than some people.

Chandler Well, piss off, then, and take your qualifications with you, you pair of talentless dykes.

Prim (*tautly*) Right. That's it. That is sexual provocation and harassment, I am going straight to the commission and I am going to have you indicted. Run the programme on your own. See how you get on.

She stomps out.

Trudi (*following her off*) Sometimes you go too far, Chance, you really do.

Trudi goes out.
A silence.

Adam (*muttering*) I think that – I think that was probably my fault.

Chandler (*quiet again now*) I used to make movies, you know.

Adam Yes, I know, I'm a great fan of –

Chandler I had this vast crew – in those days . . . Cameramen, carpenters, gaffers, electricians, best boys . . . You name it. They were all there. Assistant directors. Hundreds of assistant directors. And I'd come on the set and it'd be like God had arrived, you know . . .

26

Adam I can imagine . . .

Chandler And there'd be this silence. As they all waited for me – me! – to speak. And I'd say very quietly – I never raised my voice on the set – people listened, they wanted to listen, they wanted – even the actors – they wanted to learn – and I'd say, 'All right, people, let's go to work –' (*He pauses dramatically.*) And they'd mark the scene and I'd say – 'Action!'

Immediately, the action starts up again on the floor. The Young Man resumes crying, the Doctor moves in to examine him as Jacie steps back from the bed.

Doctor Now then, let's have a look at it, old chap, shall we? See how it's healing –

Chandler (*furiously*) Shut! Shut up! Shut up!

Doctor Oh, yes. This is really looking very healthy indeed. No worries here, nurse . . .

Chandler lunges at Prim's control panel in an attempt to stop all this.

Chandler (*as this happens*) Damn to hell! Damn it!

He finally achieves something. The dialogue stops and the Doctor exits abruptly. Rather more incongruously, the Young Man also gets out of bed and hobbles off on his one good foot.
Only Jacie remains.
Chandler and Adam stare.

Adam What did you do?

Chandler I don't know. I think I must have hit the fire alarm. What was I saying?

Adam You in the studio . . .

Chandler Oh, yes. Look at me. Now where am I?

Mechanical actors. And an entire technical department of two ball-breaking shrews. They're a pair, did you gather that?

Adam Yes, well, that's fine. I have no problem with that.

Chandler I have no problem with that. Except there's nothing in it for me. I could never quite warm to a woman when there was clearly nothing in it for me, you know. There needs to be a promise of something, however remote, don't you think so? Otherwise what's the point?

Adam No. I don't quite see it that way. But each man to his –

Chandler (*confidentially*) I tried to make it with Prim once, you know . . .

Adam Really?

Chandler Before I realized she was with Trudi. She gave me this lecture. About dignity. Respecting her dignity. I didn't do anything to her, you understand. I just said to her – you've got terrific tits, how about it? Anyway. So she gave me this lecture. When I was in the studio – the make-up girls were queuing nine deep, you know. To make it with me.

Adam Heavens.

Chandler Still. That was then. This is now. Right?

Adam Dead right.

Chandler Something to do with age, I guess. You ever seen any of my movies?

Adam I've seen them all.

Chandler Did you ever see *The Passionate Playboy*?

Adam Oh, my goodness, *The Passionate Playboy* is one of my most . . .

Chandler Some of the best comic playing ever. On screen or off screen.

Adam I agree.

Chandler And the most interesting thing is that last shot – you remember the last shot – when she comes back to him – remember it –?

Adam All in one take . . .

Chandler All in one take . . . Did you ever see that movie?

Adam Twenty-three times so far.

Chandler You need to have seen the movie to appreciate it. They're all dead now. One single take. (*He stares at the motionless Jacie*) Did you see that just now? That – thing over there. I swear it did a take. A good old-fashioned double take. Looked like it'd been watching too much James Finlayson. Do you know who I mean by James –?

Adam Yes.

Chandler Old vaudeville actor, before your time. It did a take like he used to do . . . He's dead now as well.

Adam I'm afraid that was me.

Chandler What? You mean you killed him?

Adam No, I taught her the take. I showed her how to do a double take.

Chandler When did you do that?

Adam At lunch-time.

Chandler You've got to understand about those things.

You do something, they'll copy it. You undo your zipper to scratch yourself you'll find the Doctor's doing it in the next scene. They're quite undiscriminating. They're jackdaws. They see something, hear something, they'll pick it up, they'll use it. They're recording machines on legs, that's all they are.

Adam (*indicating Jacie*) I think that one is rather more than that.

Chandler That one? It's just like all the other ones. They're all identical. Thousands of them. All identical. Different shapes and sizes but they all operate the same. They're actoids.

Adam I swear that Jacie has – a sense of humour. She laughs.

Chandler They can all laugh. It's part of the programming.

Adam No. Jacie laughs – spontaneously. She finds things funny and then she laughs.

Chandler What did you call it? Jacie?

Adam She told me that was her name. Jacie something Triplethree.

Chandler No, that's its registration number. It just told you its number.

Adam Number?

Chandler J.C. That stands for Juvenile Character, then probably F for female and then its number . . .

Adam (*disappointed*) Oh, I see.

Chandler It has no sense of humour. How can a machine have a sense of humour?

Adam I swear. (*calling*) Jacie!

Jacie Yes?

Adam Go on, tell her a joke or something. I swear she'll laugh.

Chandler You want me to tell it a joke?

Adam Yes.

Chandler All right. I say, I say, what's the secret of good comedy?

Slight pause.

Adam I don't know. Tell me what's the se—

Chandler (*interrupting him swiftly*) Timing.

Silence. Jacie frowns. Nobody laughs.

There you are. What did I tell you? It didn't laugh.

Adam It's a very old joke.

Chandler You think I'm wasting a new joke on a machine? What are you doing here anyway? You sleeping with Carla? Her entrée for the week?

Adam No, I'm really not, I'm —

Chandler What are you? Her packed lunch?

Adam No, I'm here because – I want to write.

Chandler What, you want to write soaps? Then you're out of luck. Soaps don't get written, not any more, they just happen. All we do is put in the story lines and tweak the emotions. We don't need writers. Those things are the writers, these days. Their characters are pre-programmed. Give them a subject, away they go. The miracle of modern technology. Wind 'em up and see 'em laugh, see 'em cry, they'll keep you entertained for hours, folks. The drawback, of course, is that the whole process bypasses even the smallest, most insignificant scrap of creative achievement. It's no longer a dying art, boy, it's dead. Sail away now. Save your soul.

Adam I don't want to write soaps.

Chandler You don't?

Adam No, I want to write comedy.

Chandler (*stunned*) Comedy?

Adam Yes. Real comedy. Like it used to be. Like you used to make it.

Chandler Sonny boy, didn't anybody tell you?

Adam What?

Chandler That's deader than this business. That's seriously buried. You think these things can produce comedy? You're joking. Oh, they can do funny things – if you tell them. And if you tell them right they'll be quite funny doing it, but that's all they'll do. No more. No less. And that's not comedy. That's just being funny. But comedy – you want to know about comedy?

Adam That's why I'm here . . .

Chandler Comedy is two things. First, it's surprise. You're like a magician. They're expecting this – but you give them that. Yes?

Adam Yes.

Chandler The great Oliver Hardy, he's a chimney sweep sitting in the fireplace. The whole chimney's collapsed. All the bricks are coming down, showering down on his head. He sits there letting it happen. It finishes. He looks at us. Can this be happening to me, I don't believe it? He looks up the chimney, appealing to heaven – a last brick hits him in the face. We know it's going to happen, but not when it's going to happen or, just as important, *how* it's going to happen. That's comedy.

Adam Right!

Chandler That double take you taught it. Now that's a basic double take. You can't use that, not any more. Everybody knows it. Every joker in the pub does a double take . . .

Adam Oh, I know, I was only . . .

Chandler What you have to do is look for variations . . . I love this one. I'm in here on my own, working. Suddenly, you come into the room. You're – I don't know – something's happened to you. You're –

Adam Covered in mud?

Chandler That'll do. So you come on in and just stand there. Watch this.

Adam makes as if he has entered the room. Chandler does a series of small mini-takes on Adam. Finally, he makes as if to leave the room himself and at the last moment does a final take on Adam. Jacie laughs. Chandler stares at her.

It's laughing.

Adam I know.

Chandler Why is it laughing? (*fiercely, to Jacie*) What are you laughing at?

Jacie It was funny.

Chandler (*shaking his head*) It's not possible. It's a fault, there's a flaw in it somewhere. These things are full of glitches, they're always breaking down. Why did it laugh, for God's sake?

33

Adam You heard her. She thought it was funny.

Chandler Not she. It. It's an it. It's a dishwasher. It's a floor polisher. It's a tumble dryer, that's all it is.

Adam I'd like to try and write something for her. It. In between, obviously, when you're recording. I'd like to – borrow it. Try some things out. Would that be possible? I have some ideas I'd like to try.

Chandler stares at him.

Isn't this the way you started? Someone gave you a chance? Please.

Chandler You've been here twenty minutes, you cheeky bastard.

Adam I know. If my script turned out any good – would you direct?

Chandler (*shaking his head, half-amused*) I don't believe it. Who do you think you are, coming in here like this?

Adam I'm a Trainsmith. We're an ambitious family.

Chandler (*after a pause*) You do it in your own time at your own expense, all right?

Adam Thank you.

Chandler And don't take advantage of my staff. They work their butts off as it is.

Adam Absolutely. It's a deal, then? (*He shakes Chandler's hand.*) Thank you, Mr Tate, thank you.

Chandler Chance. Call me Chance. I think I've just been conned.

Adam smiles.

I'd better go and fetch those people back. Apologize to them. Again.

Adam Has it happened before?

Chandler About once a week. I'll surprise them this time. I'll cover myself in mud.

He starts to leave.

Adam Excuse me, Chance . . .

Chandler Uh?

Adam You said that comedy was two things. The unexpected and . . . What was the other?

Chandler (*shaking his fist*) Anger.

He goes out.

Adam Did you hear all that?

Jacie Yes.

Adam We're in. We're on. We're going to do it.

Jacie Yes.

Adam Are you excited?

Jacie (*considering for a moment*) Yes. I'm excited.

Adam Then get excited.

Jacie (*jubilantly*) YES!!!!

Adam That's better. I never thought he'd say yes. But he's a rebel, you see. It's the sort of gamble that would appeal to him. They tried to sack him, did you know that? When my uncle's company took over they tried to get rid of him. He was still making quality movies at the time but they didn't want him. He wouldn't toe the line. He argued, he went over budget. That was his worst crime. He overspent. He upset the accountants. So they moved him sideways. And this is where he's been left. One of the five greats ever – in my own humble opinion.

It's a disgrace. A scandal. Don't you agree?

Jacie I think you're both similar.

Adam Really? I'd like to think that. Really?

Jacie You live for your dreams . . .

Adam That's right.

Jacie I read somewhere that dreams are merely glimpses of the reality we all could share if we only had the courage –

Adam (*rather startled*) Yes?

Jacie But we can find that courage together, can't we?

Adam Yes. You bet.

Jacie Oh, it's such an exciting dream, David . . .

A burst of music appears to emanate from her.

Adam David, who's David? I'm Adam. What's that?

Jacie I'm sorry?

Adam That music?

Jacie Oh.

The music stops as abruptly as it started.

Adam What was it? Where was it coming from?

Jacie Me.

Adam You?

Jacie It's a programme. It was intended at one time that we'd provide our own background music. But the unions objected. It's never used. Except when –

Adam When what?

Jacie Sometimes, when I produce strong emotion – joy, sadness, even anger – it just starts inside me. I can't control it. (*worriedly*) I think I have another fault.

Adam You know, I'm beginning to love your faults.

Carla enters briskly.

Carla Here I am at last. Sorry I've taken so long. I hate downsizing meetings. All those tears and recriminations. Why can't people just accept that they're no longer wanted? Bleating on about their pension schemes . . . Ready?

Adam I –

Carla I thought we'd do something really exciting this evening. I've commandeered Lester's jet. I took your name in vain, I'm afraid. I said you were dying to see the Paris operation. We can be there in time for dinner. You ready? Then in the morning, I thought I'd take you to –

Adam I'm sorry, Carla, but I think I'm going to be staying on here.

Carla What?

Adam Thank you but I've just set something up. I'm writing, you see, and I've just been promised the use of this studio so I think I need to take advantage of that, thank you all the same.

Carla You've been offered the use of this studio?

Adam In a way.

Carla By whom?

Adam Well – by Chance. Mr Tate.

Carla Chandler is an employee of this company. He can't offer the use of a studio –

37

Adam I don't want to get him into any trouble, it was just –

Carla How can he possibly offer the use of a studio? How dare he?

Adam Well . . .

Carla What do you intend to do in it? *War and Peace* or something?

Adam No, no. Just small-scale. Something I'm writing.

Carla Adam, dear, you badly need to learn the facts of television life. This is not how you go about things. If you want to make a programme, the first thing you do is submit the idea in writing to our storyline department. If they approve it, then they will pass it on to our script department. Storyline have a big backlog at present so this can take up to six months. In turn, the script department will then consider it and if they're enthusiastic – and they also have a huge backlog, so add another six months at least – they will contact you and suggest you develop your idea to what we call PFS, the Primary Full Synopsis. This is unpaid and there is no guarantee at the end of it that the idea will go forward from there. But assuming it's approved, and that's a very big if, because the competition is frightening, you will be asked to meet an editor who will talk it through with you and all being well and if they're happy, you will receive a down payment commissioning a first draft. Scripts can go to four or five drafts, generally more. This process can take anything up to two years. At the end of this time, if we can find an interested director, the piece might actually be made. Though I should warn you that for every hundred scripts that reach their final draft stage, only fifteen are made and of those usually five are shelved before transmission. And unless it's transmitted, under the new agreements, you will not, of course, receive your full and final fee. Welcome to modern television, Adam.

Adam In which case, I think I stand a better chance here.

Carla You stand no chance at all because I won't allow it to happen.

Adam Why not?

Carla Because I am the overall Regional Director here, Adam, and things are done my way. And I don't care if you're the chairman's mistress, you can bloody well toe the line like everybody else, now are you coming?

Adam In that case, I might just have to go over your head . . .

Carla I think you should know I'm very upset about this, Adam –

Adam . . . I might phone my uncle and see what he says.

Carla You're really prepared to drag Lester Trainsmith in to this?

Adam If necessary. I haven't met him for twenty years but he seems to have my interests at heart.

Carla I underestimated you. You're a pushy little bastard, aren't you?

Adam Only if I'm pushed.

Carla What is this programme, anyway?

Adam It's – not fully developed yet but – I'm writing something for Jacie.

Carla Who?

Adam Jacie. Jacie – Triplethree.

Carla Who the hell is Jacie Triplethree?

Jacie Me.

Carla (*startled*) That? You're writing for that?

Adam Yes.

Carla That's an actoid. You can't write a special for an actoid. They're only used for daytime soaps. And tiny parts. You can't use them in proper programmes.

Adam We feel that Jacie has potential.

Carla Who do?

Adam Me and Mr Tate.

Carla Rubbish! What's it ever done, for God's sake?

Jacie I've starred in some of the most successful daytime serials that have ever been produced by this network. In *The Market Girls* I played Tracy, a fun-loving teenager –

Carla Shut up!

Jacie (*unintimidated*) – who came to a tragic end when she drowned herself off Wapping Pier clasping the baby that nobody wanted her to have . . .

Carla Listen, I – Will you tell her to shut up . . .?

Adam I don't know how to shut her up.

Jacie I then went on to join the very successful *Teen Time*, where I played Marcie, the bookish frump, who was later transformed by her love for Derek into a glamorous bride. Unfortunately their marriage ended prematurely when their car overturned in Sicily.

Carla (*at the console*) Bloody machine. Cut it off! How do I cut it off?!

Jacie Next to the police series *Fair Cops* where I played Helen Dudgeon, the rookie with a sexual hang-up and a grudge – for which I received very favourable reviews despite the show's brief run . . .

Carla manages to shut off Jacie, who stops abruptly.

Carla There! (*She glares at Adam.*) And you're proposing to work with that?

Adam Yes.

Carla I thought we had an understanding between us, Adam. I'm very disappointed in you. I'm very, very upset. And hurt.

Adam I'm sorry.

Carla I thought we were . . . I took a lot of time and trouble over our arrangements tonight. That restaurant has a three-month waiting list.

Adam Well. Perhaps you should have consulted me first.

Carla I don't ask, Adam. I take. And no one says no. I don't give a stuff if you want to make a fool of yourself but don't think you can make a fool of me. Clear? (*She goes to the door. To Jacie*) And I'll have you melted down as well, you ugly little actoid.

Carla storms out, passing Chandler accompanied by Prim and Trudi.

Prim What on earth have you done to her, Adam?

Adam I'm afraid I said no.

Prim Oh dear.

Trudi She won't like that.

Prim and Trudi (*together, triumphantly*) Yeah!

Chandler She's a dangerous enemy, boy. Don't get on her dark side. (*with a glance at Jacie*) That includes you,

41

Triplethree. OK, people, let's go to work.

Jacie Yes, sir!

They stare at her for a second, surprised. Then, as they go about their tasks, the lights fade.

SCENE THREE

The same. Some days later.

We are witnessing a rehearsal of Adam's script.

Everyone is there, Chandler, Prim and Trudi all in their places with Adam hopping about nervously .

The 'cast' have undergone personality changes but, owing to their obligations to the regular series, they have made only token attempts to alter their appearance.

They include the Doctor, now playing the Farmer; the Mother, now playing the Wife, and Jacie playing herself.

The set has been moved around slightly. The bed is there together with two tables, one to represent a stove and another a kitchen table. There are also a couple of chairs.

At the start, the Farmer is bringing an unconscious Jacie into the house.

Farmer (*calling*) Mother . . . Mother . . . Quickly! Give me a hand here.

Wife (*rushing to help*) What is it, Father? What's happened?

Farmer I don't know for certain. I found her lying by the side of the road. It may have been a hit and run. Come on, get her on to the bed.

Struggling, they get Jacie to the bed and lay her down.

There! That's it!

Wife She doesn't look right.

Farmer She's not right. We may need to fetch the doctor.

Wife He's twenty mile away. He'll never get through in this snow.

Farmer Aye, true. Three metres deep it is up at Hegg's Bottom.

Wife (*to Jacie*) Are you all right, love? Can you hear me? Oh, she's that cold, poor little thing. I'll get her a rug, Father . . .

Jacie makes feeble noises, as if trying to speak.

What's she saying? (*to Jacie*) Are you trying to tell us something, love?

More noises from Jacie.

What's she trying to say, Father?

Farmer If you shut up a minute, Mother, we might be able to hear her.

They lean close to Jacie to hear.

Come on, lass, what are you trying to say?

Jacie (*speaking with difficulty*) I – fell – off – the lorry . . .

Wife What did she say?

Farmer She fell off a larry . . .

Prim Damn! Sorry!

Chandler Hold it! Hold it!

The actoids freeze, except Jacie.

Good. That's an improvement.

Jacie Was that better?

43

Chandler Much better, good. Less is beautiful, all right? Get that into your tiny tin brain, Jacie, less is better, yes?

Jacie Yes, sir.

Prim I'm sorry, Chance. I'm trying to compensate but the fault is so occasional . . .

Chandler Don't worry, Prim. Do your best. You can do no more than your best.

Prim Thank you. (*to Trudi*) He's so cheerful today.

Trudi Won't last.

Chandler Listen, clear, please – Prim, will you clear them all except Jacie?

Prim (*as she works the console*) They'll be here any moment, Chance. . .

Chandler Do it. We've got time. Keep an eye out for them, Trudi.

The Farmer and the Wife go off. So does Trudi.

You happy, Adam?

Adam The happiest man in the world.

Chandler My God. A happy author. We're in big trouble, people!

Prim I'm leaving Jacie free the whole time, Chance. Is that what you want?

Chandler We can't feed her, she's got to do her own thing. Just run the others.

Prim Right. As long as you know I'm not answerable –

Chandler Understood. (*to Jacie*) Now, listen. Don't get clever, don't get smart. You've got good instincts, and most important you've got natural timing. But when it comes to judgement, you've got to trust me a little, all right?

Jacie Yes, sir.

Chandler You notice I'm always wanting you to do a little bit less, you're always wanting to do a bit more, yes?

Jacie Yes.

Chandler You won't be the first actor to want to do that. You may be the first actoid but not the first actor. You have to learn control, yes?

Jacie Yes, sir.

Chandler You show these people today what you can do, they will be knocked out. But don't try to show off, don't pander to them in any way. Always keep the comic truth. Because once they stop believing, they go home. So you listen to me. One day you'll be a big star, you can tell me to go screw myself, but right now you're just a smart kid with potential – (*indicating Adam*) – like him. The boy genius.

Adam What did I say?

Trudi (*at the door*) There's a van pulling in.

Prim They're here, Chance.

Chandler One more thing . . .

Prim Chance, they're here . . .

Chandler (*yelling*) One damn minute!

Trudi It's all right, they still have to unload the chair . . .

Chandler OK, quickly. When you pick up the hot kettle, you know where I mean?

Jacie Yes, sir.

Chandler In a comedy, you've got a choice of ways you

can burn yourself. You can do it big, or you can do it small. You have a choice. You can pick it up like this: (*He picks up the kettle and drops it with a great yell and hops about.*) Or. Alternatively. You can choose to do it like this. (*He repeats the business. This time he replaces the kettle and walks away mouthing a silent scream.*) You know which choice I want you to make?

Jacie The little one.

Chandler Aren't I predictable? The one thing never to choose is the middle ground. (*This time he picks up the kettle and reacts with genuine pain.*) Now that hurt. You leave that till you play Saint Joan. Nobody laughs at that except sadists and weirdos and them we can do without. The other choices can still be as true but with either of them we're reassured you're not going to die from major burns. Yes?

Jacie Yes, sir.

Chandler Good. Thank you for listening to me. I am incredibly grateful. I appreciate it. I am very old and you have talent and potential which will outlive me but most of all I love you for calling me sir. (*to the others*) Who told her to call me sir?

Prim Nobody. She just decided.

Chandler I think everybody should call me sir. Why not?

Carla has entered.

Carla Good morning, sir.

Chandler Ah, Mrs Pepperbloom. Come to prejudice proceedings no doubt?

Carla I'm sure Lester is quite capable of making his own decisions. May I have your attention, everyone? Very briefly. As you know, Mr Trainsmith is incapacitated.

Although his hearing is excellent he will be conversing with you today through a third party. Please respect Mr Trainsmith's personal space and do not invade it. On no account attempt to make physical contact with Mr Trainsmith or allow any actoid within five metres of him, Mr Trainsmith has an aversion to actoids. Finally, do not try to ask him direct questions but allow Mr Trainsmith to initiate all verbal intercourse.

Chandler We will now pause for the National Anthem.

Carla Here he comes. Please rise.

> *They all get up, Chandler last of all, very reluctantly.*
> *Lester Trainsmith is wheeled in. He is well wrapped up and remains motionless throughout. Apart from the flickering of his eyelids there is little evidence that he is alive at all.*
> *Behind him is his 'Speaker', Marmion, who pushes the wheelchair. Marmion wears an earpiece, the wire of which runs down to Lester with whom it is presumably connected.*

(*consulting her wrist crib sheet*) Mr Trainsmith, may I introduce Chandler Tate, our director, whom I'm sure you remember . . .

Chandler Hi!

Carla Our programmer, Prim Spring, and our technician, Trudi Flote.

Trudi Floote

Prim Glad to meet you, Mr Trainsmith.

Carla And of course your nephew, Adam, whom I'm sure needs no introduction.

Adam Well, I don't know, it has been twenty years. How are you, uncle?

47

Chandler (*growling*) Don't ask direct questions . . .

Carla Finally, Marmion, who will introduce himself.

Marmion Good afternoon, everybody, my name is Marmion Çedilla and I shall be serving as Speaker for Mr Trainsmith today. Although he can hear perfectly, all his speech will be re-routed through the medium of myself. I would therefore ask you from now onwards to treat everything I say as coming from Mr Trainsmith himself. If I should need to interpolate personally at any time I will always identify myself to avoid any confusion. Finally, from now on, please try to ignore me entirely and to address all your remarks to Mr Trainsmith himself and to treat all replies as if they were coming from him directly. Thank you for your attention.

Chandler (*to Prim*) It's a talking pink blancmange.

Prim Shh!

Carla Shall we get going, everyone? I'm afraid our schedule is running very behind so we're going to have to make this very quick.

Chandler It's a half-hour excerpt, what are we supposed to do? Run it at double speed?

Carla Shorten it.

Chandler Shorten it? By how much.

Carla Five minutes?

Chandler Yes, I guess we can shorten it by five minutes.

Carla No. To five minutes. We have time to see just five minutes.

Chandler What the hell can we show you in five minutes?

Marmion (*sharply*) That's all you've got. Now get on with it.

Chandler (*looking at Marmion, startled*) What? (*looking at Trainsmith*) Oh, right. Five minutes. OK. What are we going to do in five minutes?

Adam I could perhaps try and describe the overall idea.

Chandler Good, yes. OK. I'll find a little piece to show. (*to Carla*) Come on, give us a break, what can we show in five minutes?

Carla (*smiling*) I'm afraid that's all you have.

Chandler God, you're vengeance on wheels, aren't you? The kid's first script and you –

Adam (*swiftly*) Well, very quickly, the idea is this. It's a comedy. It's unusual in that it's a full-length, a one-off, two-hour special –

Carla (*laughing*) Oh, forget that . . .

Adam Though I do envisage that this could be a full-length pilot and that if it was successful, spin-offs, a series, a half-hour series could be developed, using the main characters.

Carla Two hours? Please. Who's going to be awake after two hours?

Adam If I may finish –?

Carla We have trouble with twenty minutes.

Adam Please, you have given us five minutes. Allow me to have them, please.

Marmion Shut up and let him speak, Carla.

Adam Thank you. Our central character in this story is Jacie. She is a –

Marmion Did you say Jacie?

Adam Yes.

Marmion How do you spell it?

Adam (*rather loudly, to Trainsmith*) J – A – C – I – E . . .

Marmion You don't have to shout, I can hear you.

Adam Sorry. Anyway, the story is –

Marmion Did you know there was once a famous female comedian called Gracie?

Adam Yes, Gracie Allen. Used to be with George Burns. I don't know them that well, but I've seen footage . . .

Marmion I'm almost old enough to remember her first time around. (*sotto*) That's a joke.

Adam laughs briefly.

If she's half as funny as Gracie Allen, we've got a hit.

Adam I hope so. Anyway. Jacie is an actoid. The joke is, she's an actoid playing an actoid. Which as far as I know's never been done before –

Carla Hilarious.

Adam And she's just come out of the factory and she's being transported to the studio, absolutely brand new, unused. And it's winter, there's heavy snow and the lorry is crossing the Pennine Hills, very treacherous, when it skids and the driver momentarily loses control. The actoid, Jacie, falls out of the lorry. Her box smashes, she rolls clear and is lying by the side of the road where she's discovered by Jethro, a farmer who's been rounding up his sheep in the blizzard. Jethro brings Jacie to his cottage where he and his wife revive her, accidentally activating her. Being simple people they don't realize that Jacie is an actoid. Moreover when she wakes up, because she has no memories, just her basic factory programming, *she* doesn't realize she's an actoid. She thinks they're her parents. Failing to trace her real parents, they bring her up as the child they never had. She's very quick, she's clever and soon she's reading every book she can lay her hands on. She's fun, she's popular, she has a clear, unclouded wisdom. Being an actoid she's also physically very strong. She makes a lot of friends especially among the young. In the local community, which is rife with corrupt business deals, backstabbings and sexual betrayals, she shines like an innocent. She becomes the local hero. She's like a latter-day superman. She rescues a child from a burning building, she talks a gunman into giving himself up and so on and so on. Eventually, the grateful local people elect her as mayor.

Carla They make an *actoid* their mayor?

Adam Yes, but they don't know she is, that's the point. But unfortunately, she has made enemies. In particular a jealous local woman, a leading councillor, who believes that Jacie stole her husband from her. This councillor finds out about Jacie's past, makes enquiries, and on the eve of the election, she exposes her as an actoid. The people are furious that they've been duped into voting for a machine. They turn on Jacie, driving her out, stoning her. Failing to kill her, they leave her by the side of the road in the snow once again. Waiting for someone to rescue her once more. In search of another adventure.

He pauses. A silence.

That's the basic story.

Carla It's supposed to be a comedy?

Adam It's funny, yes, but it's also – I don't know . . .

Chandler It's a comedy. That doesn't mean everyone has to be falling in bowls of custard, for God's sake. It's an allegory. It's a satire . . .

Carla I can see the ratings rocketing through the roof already . . .

Chandler What would you know, you hard-boiled ball-crusher?

Prim Chance!

Chandler You only came in here to sink it. That's all you're ever looking to do –

Carla It doesn't need any help from me, darling –

Marmion You're wasting my time. Show me a little of the treatment.

Chandler (*calming down*) All right. (*He pauses to pull himself together.*)

Prim (*indicating the script, softly to Chandler*) Perhaps we could show them this little bit, Chance?

Carla You've got one and a half minutes left.

Chandler (*resignedly*) Oh, show them that bit. What difference does it make? She's pissed on it and drowned it anyway. (*He sits sulkily.*)

Prim This is early on – a part of what we rehearsed and it's when Jacie first wakes up in her new home. The farmer and his wife have taken turns to sit by her bed. It is nearly dawn and the farmer has fallen asleep.

> *Jacie has got back on to the bed. The Farmer has re-entered, pulled up a chair by the bed and fallen asleep. Prim looks at Chandler.*

Chandler All right, people, let's go to work. Action.

> *Jacie wakes up. She sits up. She looks around her. She looks puzzled. She studies the room and gingerly lowers her legs over the side of the bed. She stares at the*

Farmer who is snoring gently.

(*to Prim, softly*) Lower the snoring, less snoring.

The Farmer's snoring lessens. Jacie approaches him. She puts her hand tentatively to his face. He grunts. She withdraws her hand. She moves to the table. There is a note on it and a dish covered with a cloth.

Jacie (*reading*) Father. If she wakes up, give her some of this to eat, love, Mother. (*She looks puzzled.*) Mother? (*looking at the Farmer*) Father? (*as it dawns on her*) Father!

She smiles. The Farmer sleeps on. Jacie lifts the cloth covering the dish. It is a sort of egg custard. She tastes it on her finger approvingly. She moves to the stove. She examines it. She reaches out and tries to pick up the kettle. It is hot. She does the discreet take that Chandler taught her.

Chandler Good! Good!

Carla No, that needs to be bigger, surely? That needs to be bigger if it's ever going to be funny.

Chandler glares at her. Jacie, still staring at her hand, accidentally walks into the table. The noise arouses the Farmer who wakes up, startled. He stares at Jacie. She stares at him. A silence.

Jacie (*tentatively*) Father?

Farmer (*puzzled*) Father?

Jacie Father! (*running to him*) Oh, father.

She embraces him. He responds, rather bewildered. The Wife enters and stops as she sees this.

Wife Father?

Farmer (*a little embarrassed*) Oh. Mother.

Jacie (*turning to the Wife, overjoyed*) Mother? Oh, mother!

She runs and embraces the Wife who is equally confused. Over Jacie's shoulder she looks enquiringly at the Farmer, who shrugs helplessly.

Chandler Cut!

Marmion Bravo! (*He claps.*)

Adam You like it, uncle?

Marmion No, I'm sorry, that was me. I should have identified myself. Mr Trainsmith – I am now he – I feel it has a certain potential . . .

Chandler You bet it has potential. Your nephew is good, Mr Trainsmith. He has that great comic writer's gift – economy. That whole scene there – simple, touching, funny. With how many – two, three words?

Carla May I also add, sentimental, cloying, under-energized and totally unreal.

Chandler Unreal? What do you mean, unreal?

Adam I think that's being very unfair . . .

Carla Well, maybe in the right hands it could be quite charming . . .

Chandler We weren't looking for charming –

Carla Well, you should be, Chandler, because currently charming is in, dear. That's what our viewers are looking for –

Adam How can you judge anything from a one-minute scene –?

Marmion I wish to make a point here –

Carla (*ignoring him*) It's been done on less, darling, I can tell you. *Madly Moving Parts* was commissioned from half a page of foolscap.

Chandler And what a load of crap that was –

Marmion Would you all listen to me for a –

Adam (*incredulously*) *Madly Moving Parts* . . .?

Carla The first Christmas Special – thirty-one million. A twenty-five million average over forty-eight weeks –

Marmion This is Mr Trainsmith speaking . . .

Chandler (*losing it completely*) So what does that prove? There are thirty-one million people who get blind drunk at Christmas and don't give a shit –

Carla Including you, I have no doubt . . .

Marmion I'm insisting you calm down at once or I'll –

Adam Could we just talk about this quietly, please?

Chandler (*furiously*) What do you know? What do you know about anything at all? You're an accountant! How can you appreciate anything? How can you be moved by anything? You wouldn't know a piece of art if it came up and screwed you from the rear. How can you even get an erection, for Christ's sake, if you never take your head out of a ledger . . .?

Carla Thank you but I don't happen to have such things.

Chandler Well, you could have fooled me, baby!

Prim (*jumping up and yelling*) Would you all please shut up, shut up, SHUT UP!

  A silence.

Marmion Could we list –

Prim (*sharply*) Shut up! (*realizing who she has shouted at*) Oh, I'm sorry, Mr Trainsmith. (*indicating Marmion*) I meant him. Not you.

Marmion Could we listen to people one at a time, starting with Mrs Pepperbloom.

Carla Thank you so much, Mr Trainsmith. (*very calmly*) All I am saying is, as Regional Director, I'm prepared to take this project downline but there are a lot of things that have to be talked about first.

Chandler When did we ever say –?

Prim Shhh!

Carla I would want two, preferably three experienced writers to go through the synopsis with Adam and get it into some sort of working shape.

Adam It is in some sort of . . . (*He tails away.*)

Carla But there is no way we can consider a two-hour project. In case you haven't been around, two-hour projects have been dead a very long time indeed. We downshape it to eighteen minutes thirty-five seconds including credits and maybe we try it as a late-night/early morning art slot. That is all I can promise.

Adam Oh, great . . .

Chandler Hooray! We made the art slot . . .

Carla But. Wait! Hear me out. None of this can happen until we have solid casting commitment. (*standing by Jacie*) We need that name, darlings. If we're to sell it on, we need a household in this role.

Adam Well, that's out of the question.

Carla Then so's the programme, Adam, I'm sorry. That is not negotiable.

Adam The whole thing was written around Jacie . . . It's written with her in –

Carla Darling, look at it. Just take a look at it. Are you seriously proposing I go out and try and market a programme based on *that*?

Adam Why not?

Carla Adam, it's an actoid. A run-of-the-mill, daytime-TV, supporting-unit actoid. It's not even a grade A. You cannot build a programme round this – I mean, just look at it. It can't walk, it can barely talk and it has all the personality of a meat safe.

> *Some rather menacing music is heard. It appears to be coming from Jacie.*

Now, it might be that there are half a dozen viewers somewhere in the world – (*hearing the music*) what's that music? – somewhere in the world who are prepared to sit down and waste eighteen minutes thirty-five seconds of their busy lives watching a piece of scrap metal cavorting around with about as much sex appeal as a tin of corned beef but I'm not – gluuurrrp!

> *Jacie has picked up the dish of egg custard from the table and squashed it in Carla's face. She twists the plate in the way she has been taught. Carla stands stunned for a moment.*

Chandler (*softly*) Oh, my God . . .

> *For the first time, a sound emanates from Lester himself. It is the very rusty sound of laughter. Marmion, after a second, registers this and begins to laugh on his master's behalf.*

*Chandler, Prim, Trudi and finally Adam all start
laughing. Jacie looks at them, pleased with the reaction.
She, too, starts laughing.*

*Carla starts to remove the gunge from her eyes. Trudi
goes to her and tries to take her arm.*

Trudi Let me show you the bathroom, Mrs –

*Carla shakes her off and stalks out. Trudi follows her,
untroubled by this.*

The laughter subsides.

Marmion Thank you for that, I haven't laughed that
much for years.

Adam She can be funnier than that, uncle, you should see
her.

Prim What about the programme, Mr Trainsmith? I'm
sorry that's a direct question, only –

Marmion I'm prepared to go ahead with the programme
on the terms and conditions outlined by Mrs Pepperbloom.

Adam But, uncle, what about Jacie?

Lester (*speaking with difficulty*) Melt her down.

Marmion (*repeating him, rather unnecessarily*) Melt her
down.

Lester indicates and Marmion starts to wheel him out.

Adam You can't melt her down, she's a – she's a person.

Marmion (*over his shoulder as they go*) She's unstable,
next time she could kill someone . . .

A silence.

Adam This is all my fault. It's my fault.

Chandler Did you teach her that as well? The custard pie?

Adam Yes.

Chandler Pretty good. It just cost us the programme, but pretty good.

Prim But Mr Trainsmith said –

Chandler I know what he said but he won't be around. She will. The Merry Widow. She's the one we have to deal with.

Adam What are we going to do? I'm not just dumping Jacie.

Chandler (*opening a drawer*) I know what I'm going to do. I suggest you do the same. (*He bangs a bottle of Scotch on the table.*) Help yourselves. Me, I'm going out for a while. This room stinks of executives. (*to Jacie, angrily*) As for you. How many times do I have to tell you, don't go over the top, you stupid fucking actor?

Adam Do you want me to come with you –

Chandler (*as he goes*) I drink alone. Didn't they tell you? (*He leaves.*)

Jacie (*to herself, pleased*) He called me an actor.

Adam Well. That's that, I suppose.

Prim You can still work on the programme. It isn't dead yet. If Mr Trainsmith is prepared to back it . . .

Adam (*indicating Jacie*) Not without her. There's no programme without her. That's final.

Prim Yes, I know it's very good. It's wonderful. But there are others, Adam, there's always someone else. Different perhaps, but just as good.

Adam I'm not doing it without Jacie.

Prim (*gently*) Adam, it's an actoid. That's all it is.

Adam She's more than that.

Prim Look, when Trudi comes back I'll get her to strip it down for you. She can peel its outer casing off, you can see for yourself. It's just a lot of wires and circuits and micro-servos and – bits. In no way is it a person. And it's actually quite bad for you to think of it as a person, Adam. It's called actoid empathy. It happens. When we do our basic staff training, we do a day on dealing with actoids. Always refer to them as it, never as he or she. Never converse with them except strictly in the line of work. Never, never socialize. As soon as you've finished with them, switch them off. Otherwise you risk getting emotionally involved, you get all screwed up and you also screw them up and then you don't know where you are –

Adam But if you'd heard her talking to me. The things she says –

Prim What it talks about, Adam – the words it uses – its so-called conversation – that's merely an amalgam of all the conversations of all the characters it's played in all the shows it's ever been in. Its personality is nothing more than that. Every time you speak to it, you trigger some response. It pulls it out of its memory bank and blurts it back at you. That's all it's doing.

Adam Maybe that's all any of us do.

Prim If I thought you really felt that, I'd think a lot less of you. I really would.

Trudi returns.

How is she?

Trudi Not a pretty sight. Where's he gone?

60

Prim The usual.

Trudi Break time, then?

Prim Might as well. (*to Adam*) Want to join us? (*Pause.*) Adam?

Adam No, I'll stay and have a drink.

Prim Don't get like him. It raises more problems than it solves, I tell you.

Carla enters, rather red-eyed from her ordeal.

Oh, Mrs –

Carla I am closing this place down. I thought you should know. Start looking around, my children, because I am closing it down.

She goes.

Trudi And a Happy New Year.

Prim I can always go back to children's programmes, I suppose. They're constantly asking me. Remember what I said, Adam, I'm serious. Don't even speak to it.

Trudi See you later.

They go.

Adam (*half to himself*) Bye. (*After a second, he looks at the bottle of Scotch. He picks it up, opens Chandler's drawer again and fishes out a glass. He is about to pour himself one.*) Would you like one? Or –

Jacie Sure. A man should never drink alone.

Adam Right. (*finding another glass*) I just had a thought. Why should you need a drink?

Jacie I drink.

Adam Yes?

61

Jacie And I eat.

Adam You do?

Jacie The sort of shows I do, we're required to eat and drink a lot.

Adam Yes.

Jacie They're all eating and drinking.

Adam Really. Cheers.

Jacie Cheers.

Adam Does the nurse eat? I mean your character as the nurse?

Jacie No, Bridget drinks. She's a secret alcoholic.

Adam Is she?

Jacie That's why I gave her the laugh, you know. With the doctor. I thought she could be drunk on duty.

Adam (*laughing*) Whose idea was that? To make her an alcoholic?

Jacie Mine. She was very boring otherwise. She just stood and nodded a lot.

Adam I see.

Pause.

How do you – this is a personal question, you don't have to answer it if you find it too personal – but what happens to all the food and the drink when you've finished with it? If you see what I mean?

Jacie Someone comes along and empties me.

Adam Stupid question. Obviously.

Pause.

Adam What did he mean by melt you down? What did he mean?

Jacie Melt down? That's when you're returned to the factory and they erase your memory and then reboot with the basic programme. I would be like Jacie in your play if that happened. I would start again.

Adam (*sipping his whisky*) Hey, this is strong. (*He coughs.*) More?

Jacie Keep 'em coming, kid.

Adam (*laughing*) And what show does that come out of? Keep 'em coming, kid? Honestly!

Jacie Episode nineteen, scene four, line twelve of *Some Dark Alley*. I was an undercover policewoman. Josie. She was shot. It was a good death scene. (*instantly in the scene, in great pain*) 'Help me, Jason, help me. You mean more to me than I've ever been able to – tell – you . . . I'm sorry . . .' It was a good scene.

Adam I don't want you melted down. I think that would be criminal.

Jacie No. No crime. Not for an actoid.

Adam All your memory gone. All you are. Wouldn't that upset you?

Jacie I've nothing I care to remember. Well, the last few days maybe.

Adam That's terribly sad. It makes me feel like crying. You wouldn't mind if Jacie – the person you are now – just ceased to exist?

Jacie I'd never know, would I? How could I mind?

She reaches out and gently strokes his head.

(*softly*) Cry if you want to.

He looks up at her. A moment between them, then he moves away.

Adam No, sitting here feeling sorry for myself is not the way. Come on, let's – I don't know. What shall we do? Go out and eat? No, that'd be no fun for you, would it? What do you want to do?

Jacie Dance.

Adam Dance?

Jacie I want to dance. I never get to dance.

Adam All right. If that's what you want. Music? How do we get music, do you know?

Jacie In that drawer. There's his collection of disks.

Adam opens a drawer.

Adam Hey, yes! Wow! Another treasure trove. These you have loved. I'm not a good dancer. I have to warn you. Are you a good dancer?

Jacie Yes. I have a programme.

Adam I somehow thought you would. Now, what's this? Zed Zed Top? Who are they? Let's try Zed Zed Top, then.

He puts the disk into the panel. The sound of ZZ Top's 'My Head's in Mississippi' booms out.

Yes? What about this?

Jacie It's good. It's funny.

She begins to move. Gently at first. Adam joins her.

Adam Hey, you do dance, don't you?

Jacie I dance.

It is apparent from the start that she is going to run

rings round him but he keeps it up gamely for a bit until her programme kicks into gear and she goes into overdrive. At the finish, Adam is left sitting breathless watching her admiringly.

I'm sorry. Are you all right?

Adam (*breathless still*) God, you're beautiful. You're so beautiful.

She smiles and offers him her hand. She helps him to his feet. We get some idea of her strength from the effortless way she does this.
They stand holding each other for a second.
Adam kisses her gently. She responds.
Music starts again, this time from Jacie. Very romantic. A love theme.

Adam Is that you?

Jacie Yes, I'm sorry. Shall I stop it?

Adam No. It's fine. It goes with the scene.

They dance a little, gently this time.

Jacie Adam, I don't want to be melted down. I don't want to forget this.

Adam Nobody's going to melt you down, I promise.

Jacie Promise?

Adam I promise.

Jacie Oh, Adam . . .

Adam Jacie . . .

Jacie Adam . . .

The music continues as the lights fade to:
Blackout.

65

Act Two

SCENE ONE

The studio.
Essentially the same, though because the locations tend to switch fairly rapidly from now on, we see a lot less of the studio area than previously in order to facilitate swift cross-cutting.
The lights come up on Chandler, Prim and Trudi.

Chandler Gone? What do you mean, they've gone?

Prim Both of them. Just taken off.

Chandler Where, for God's sake?

Prim I don't know.

Chandler What the hell's Adam playing at? He can't just elope with an actoid. It's company property. If anything happens to it we'll be paying it off for the rest of our lives. Those things are worth thousands.

Trudi One point seven million.

Chandler Thank you. What happens when – *that* much? – what happens when Carla finds out? Because she certainly will do.

Prim We'll have to find them first.

Chandler Come on, they could be anywhere in the city.

Trudi We can put out a trace.

Chandler Trace?

Trudi A security trace. Jacie'll show up sooner or later.

Prim On the screen. Every actoid leaves an individual signal.

Chandler And what if someone else gets the signal before we do?

Prim Impossible. I have the encoder.

Chandler Then trace it. Fast. (*He starts to leave. A sudden thought*) We have no nurse! We need the nurse for this afternoon's recording.

Trudi (*indicating Prim*) She can do it.

Prim Who can?

Trudi You can.

Prim Me? I'm not doing it.

Trudi I'll do the programming, Chance can go on cameras.

Chandler Good thinking. I'll shoot from behind. Just do your hair at the back.

Prim I'm not playing a nurse.

Trudi (*slyly*) You like it enough sometimes.

Prim (*rather coyly*) Stop that.

Chandler Listen, you two. You fancy playing prisoners and warders instead? Get yourself a uniform and find that actoid.

Trudi and Prim go off.

(*as he follows them*) Jesus, Adam, what are you doing to me?

As he goes, the lights cross fade to:

SCENE TWO

The foyer of the Grand Hotel.
   Distant tinkling piano music. A Desk Clerk is at reception. Adam and Jacie enter rather awkwardly. Jacie, who has never left the studio before, is in some sort of wonderland.
   They approach the desk.

Desk Clerk Good evening, sir – madam. Welcome to the Grand Hotel. May I help you at all?

Adam Yes, indeed. My – my – secretary called a few minutes ago. She made a reservation for us . . .

Desk Clerk Yes, sir. What name would that be, sir?

Adam Er – Mr and Mrs Hornblower.

Desk Clerk Hornblower. Just one moment, sir. (*He moves away and punches at the computer.*)

Adam (*sotto, to Jacie*) Why did you have to call us that? It's a ridiculous name. Hornblower.

Jacie It was the first name I thought of. I was in the series. I played the woman the Captain meets when he comes ashore at –

Desk Clerk Here we are, sir. Sorry to keep you. A double room for three nights minimum.

Adam That's the one.

Desk Clerk Would you care to register here, sir? Just the name and address will suffice.

Adam Certainly.

Desk Clerk Thank you, sir. You have luggage with you, sir?

68

Adam (*who only has his briefcase*) Er – no. We had a – a slight – a slight . . .

Desk Clerk (*suspiciously*) I see. You have no luggage?

Jacie (*switching in to some long-forgotten episode*) We've had this terrible time, you've no idea. My sister was arrested in Spain, you see, as a suspected heroin trafficker in a clear case of mistaken identity and my husband and I flew out to plead for her but when we arrived we found she'd already been released from prison and subsequently kidnapped by the real drug traffickers who suspected she'd double-crossed them. And we spent all our available money tracking them down to a rented house in northern Barcelona but all we found was her poor bullet-ridden body. And before we could do anything the police arrived and this time we were arrested for her murder. And we were in prison for four days before they believed us and we've had to travel home in just the clothes we were standing up in. It's been absolutely horrible.

Adam is staring at her incredulously.

Desk Clerk Good gracious. I am so sorry to hear that, Mrs Hornblower. How dreadful for you.

Jacie And then on top of that my husband has just found out he's only got three –

Adam (*swiftly*) Yes, well, we don't need to share all our problems at once, do we, darling? Can we go straight up?

Desk Clerk Yes, of course, sir. The fourth floor. It's a very quiet room.

Adam Thank you.

Desk Clerk Will you be paying by credit exchange?

Adam Cash.

Desk Clerk Cash?

Adam I always pay cash.

Jacie Ever since we –

Adam Ever since – an earlier incident which we won't go into now.

Desk Clerk And will Mrs Hornblower be happy to remain in her nurse's uniform?

Adam Oh, yes, yes. They lent her that when we – were body searched. Ripped her clothes to shreds. Bastards! Do you have a dress shop?

Desk Clerk There's an exclusive boutique just along the concourse there, sir. It's open until eight. I'm sure you'll find everything you need, should you wish to replenish your wardrobe.

Adam All right, darling? Shall we go shopping?

Jacie (*smiling delightedly*) Yes, you bet, darling.

Adam (*as they go*) Tell me, do you have a story for every single occasion?

They move off. Jacie's fresh persona seems to dictate that she hold Adam's hand and skip along beside him. The lights cross fade to:

SCENE THREE

The studio.
Chandler enters, followed by a furious Carla. Prim trails behind anxiously.

Carla Are you telling me, Chandler, that you have let that boy run off with company property?

Chandler Don't panic, we'll get them back.

Carla You certainly will. This amounts to grand theft. If this was anyone other than Lester's nephew, I'd call the police in straightaway.

Prim Oh no, please, there's no need for that –

Carla (*as she goes*) I'm going to make damn sure that you are held responsible for this, Chandler –

Prim Please, Mrs Pepperbloom . . .

Carla (*savagely, to Prim*) And you as well! (*Exits.*)

Chandler Where the hell are they, Prim? Why haven't you traced them?

Prim They may be somewhere shielded. We just have to wait till we get a clear signal. Trudi's up there on the roof trying to boost it.

Chandler Is that going to work?

Prim I don't know, do I?

Chandler Well, thank you, Stanley. Call me if Ollie falls off the roof, will you? (*He starts to go out.*)

Prim What's wrong with you? I thought all this would excite you. You're supposed to be the rebel round here, aren't you?

Chandler I'm still a rebel. I'm ready to fight them all, don't you worry. It's just that I have a pension to consider. I'm going for some refreshment. Don't try to follow me.

He goes. Prim sighs and follows him out.
 The lights cross fade to:

SCENE FOUR

The hotel boutique.
  Adam is waiting for Jacie. He still has his briefcase.
Similarly waiting for his girlfriend is the Man. He is rich
and very bored.
  The Girl comes out from the cubicle. She is the perfect
cut-glass partner for the Man. She wears a skimpy outfit.

Girl What do you think?

Man I think that's amazing. Absolutely startling. I should
buy that one.

Girl (*stands surveying herself for a minute*) No, I don't
like it. In fact, I hate it. I loathe and detest it. The more I
look at it. It's vile. And it's badly finished.

Man (*disappointed again*) Oh, really? Oh, dear.

  The Girl goes back in to the cubicle passing the
  Assistant on the way.

Assistant Oh, that's lovely, madam . . .

Girl (*ungraciously*) No, it isn't, it's detestable.

  Jacie comes out from her cubicle rather tentatively. She
  is wearing a very brief sun dress.

Assistant Oh, yes! And what does sir think of this one,
then?

  Jacie stands looking at Adam, anxious for his approval.

(*helpfully*) It's very attractive on her, surely?

Jacie Is this not right either?

Adam Yes, yes. It's terrific. It's just – not quite right for
dinner, you see, Jacie.

72

Assistant Oh, I'm sorry. I understood it was for a world cruise.

Adam No, no, that's later. Much later, darling.

Assistant In that case, I think we have something rather more suitable for madam.

Adam Try one more, darling.

Jacie (*in a panic, sotto to Adam*) Will you come in there with me, please?

Adam (*sotto*) I can't come in there.

Jacie She keeps making me wear things I don't want to wear . . .

Adam Well, you don't have to do that – (*to the Assistant*) – excuse us – you don't have to wear things she wants you to wear, you wear things you want to wear –

Jacie But I don't know what I want to wear. I don't know how to do this. I've never played this scene before. I just get given things to wear by the wardrobe department . . .

Adam Just choose something you feel good in.

Jacie I don't feel good in anything. (*despairingly, louder*) I don't want to wear any clothes at all . . .

The Man and the Assistant look at her, rather startled.

Adam Jacie! (*He smiles at the others.*) Come on, pull yourself together. Now, you go back in there and you choose a dress that you like, all right?

Jacie But I want to choose one you like.

Adam If you like it, I'll like it. Now take that dress off and choose another one.

Jacie Yes. (*She makes to remove her dress there and then.*)

Adam No!

Assistant Madam, please. In here, if you don't mind. (*ushering Jacie off, to Adam*) She's so eager, isn't she?

Adam Yes.

Jacie and the Assistant go off.

Man (*to Adam*) I should take a seat. You might be here for ages. I've been here since three twenty. It's now ten past seven. In that time, we've achieved one pair of tights and some shoes she thinks she'll probably come back and change later.

Adam Ah.

Man My record's four days. That was a hat for a wedding. Then she got a cold and we never went anyway.

The Girl comes out in another outfit. She stands scowling at herself.

Girl I hate my bottom. I hate it, hate it. And I loathe my thighs. They're obscene. And my shoulders are uneven. And my stomach is gross.

Man Apart from that, it's OK, is it?

Girl No, this is dreadful. I wouldn't be seen dead in it.

Man Oh, well . . .

Jacie comes out of the cubicle. She is wearing a long dress bag. Open at the bottom, it is zipped up to her neck. Her arms are trapped inside the bag. The Assistant hurries after her, agitatedly.

Jacie (*despairing*) What about this, then? Is this any good?

Girl Good heavens!

Man Wow!

Adam Jacie!

Jacie (*panicked*) This is all I can find, this is the only thing I look right in.

Assistant Madam, please, that's a dress bag . . .

Jacie (*excitedly*) It's what I'm wearing!

Assistant It's a dress bag, sir. Madam can't possibly –

Adam Yes, I can see what it is! (*taking Jacie by the shoulders, firmly*) Jacie, Jacie . . . Jacie!

Jacie (*calming down a little*) What? What?

Adam All right. Calm down. I'll choose with you. May I go in and choose with her?

Assistant (*wearily*) Please, sir. Please do.

Adam Come on, Jacie. Back we go, together. (*He leads her back to the cubicle.*)

Jacie There's so many things to choose from . . .

Adam We'll find something, don't worry . . .

  They go off.

Assistant Oh lord, what a day . . . (*She goes off after them.*)

Girl Extraordinary woman. Did you see what she was wearing?

Man I thought she looked rather good. Why don't you try one on? (*He laughs at his own rapier wit.*)

Girl (*looking at him scornfully*) You really are absolutely no help at all, are you? You're utterly useless. I don't know why I bring you. (*She goes back into the cubicle.*)

Man Nor do I.

He goes off. The lights cross fade to:

SCENE FIVE

The studio.
Chandler is pacing about looking at his watch. Prim
enters in a nurse's uniform. She is carrying her coat which
she struggles into during the scene.

Chandler Well?

Prim Got it. Clear signal. I'm locked on. Just pray they
stay put for a while.

Chandler All right, let's go.

Prim No. Not you. On my own. This needs to be handled
gently, Chance, and I'm sorry I don't trust you to do that.

Chandler If you're frightened I might punch him on the
jaw, that's possible.

Prim There is a real danger they may have fallen in love.

Chandler You're joking?

Prim Adam certainly might have done and if Jacie recip-
rocates, then I don't know what will happen.

Chandler They won't be the first people to fall in love,
for God's sake.

Prim No, but she may well be the first machine to fall in
love, that's the point.

Chandler Great! Another British first.

Prim Chance, most of us are born pre-conditioned for
love. We are subconsciously, emotionally braced from the

cradle for love to happen to us at some point in our lives. It's still one hell of a shock to our system when it comes but at least we're half prepared. Jacie is in no way prepared. Can you imagine what love would do to her? Love is a totally illogical process. Every neurological circuit in her head will be in conflict. She'll probably self destruct ... (*turning to go*) I'll keep in touch.

Chandler You going dressed like that?

Prim (*as she goes*) There's no time to lose.

Chandler (*to himself*) I know I am about to lose my pension.

   Chandler follows her worriedly as the lights fade to:

SCENE SIX

The hotel restaurant.
   Two tables are visible, both empty at present.
   Waiter 2 hovers.
   In a second, Waiter 1 enters and leads Adam and Jacie to a table. She is wearing her new dress somewhat self-consciously though, if truth be told, she's looking quite beautiful.
   Waiter 2 springs into action and they all go through the seating ritual.

Waiter 1 This all right for you, sir?

Adam Thank you very much.

Waiter 1 Madam ...

Jacie Thank you.

Waiter 1 Would you care for a drink before your meal?

Adam – Er ...

77

Jacie Yes, I'll have a Kiss-me-Quick Highball, please, with plenty of soda water, four dashes of curaçao but easy on the Pernod.

Waiter 1 (*very unflapped*) Certainly, madam. Sir?

Adam I'll – I'll just have a glass of white wine, please.

Waiter 1 Dry, sir?

Adam Please.

Waiter 1 May I leave you with the menus?

Adam Thank you.

Jacie Excuse me.

Waiter 1 Madam?

Jacie Do you like this dress? Do you think it's all right?

Waiter 1 It's – enchanting, madam.

Jacie Thank you.

Waiter 1 departs.

Adam You don't need to keep asking people, I've told you it's fine.

Jacie I want to look good for you.

Adam It doesn't matter. Honestly.

Jacie (*flaring*) Of course it matters.

Adam All right. Calm down.

Jacie I've never been in a restaurant before. Well, only one on set. But then they usually put everything in afterwards so you might as well be sitting in a box. The walls and things here, they're so beautiful. The lights. And the floor – and the ceiling – just look at that ceiling. Oh, Adam, this is so exciting.

Adam Well, enjoy it.

Jacie I will. I promise. Every second.

Waiter 1 returns with the Man and the Girl. They sit at the other table, talking softly and frequently glancing over at Adam and Jacie.

It's that couple from the dress shop. They're staring at me. Do I look all right?

Adam Stop it, now. They're looking at you because you look wonderful.

Waiter 2 arrives with their drinks. Jacie's drink is in a highball glass and elaborately decorated.

Waiter 2 Highball for madam.

Adam (*observing the size of it*) Grief.

Waiter 2 And a dry white wine, sir.

Adam Thank you.

Jacie Thank you. This is a new dress.

Waiter 2 Very nice, madam.

Waiter 2 leaves.

Jacie (*holding up her glass*) This is much better designed than the one I had before.

Adam When did you have –? Oh no, don't bother.

Jacie I never got to finish it either. I was half-way through it and then I was kidnapped and driven into the mountains and chained to a bed.

Adam Wonderful.

Jacie You don't want to hear?

Adam Not at the moment. I can't compete with your past

life, Jacie, I'm sorry. I fell off my bicycle when I was six. I think that was it.

Pause.

Jacie I don't know what else to talk about. All I have is my past life.

Adam I'm sorry. What happened in the end, then?

Jacie In the end? My brother refused to pay the ransom because he stood to inherit. It turned out he'd planned it all in the first place. They dropped me down a well. I drowned. (*a little sadly*) I'm always getting killed.

Adam Not any more. (*raising his glass*) To us.

Jacie (*tenderly*) To the way you look tonight. To the way I'll always feel. To the life we'll . . . always share.

Silence.

(*sadly, a little ashamed*) That's someone else's line as well, I'm sorry. Give me a hundred years, I may come up with something of my own.

Adam (*trying to change the mood*) Hell, we're all of us full of lines by other people. Who's original these days?

Jacie You are.

Adam You wait. By the time I've finished, you're going to be a big star.

Jacie (*unconvinced*) Yep.

They drink. Jacie drains her highball in one.

Adam Jacie!

Jacie Mmm?

Adam Doesn't matter.

Jacie 'Licious.

Adam I'm starving. Let's make some choices. (*opening his menu*) Mmm. This looks promising. See anything you fancy?

Jacie You order for me.

Adam You sure?

Jacie Please.

Adam Don't you want to look, choose for yourself?

Jacie (*opening the menu for a second, then closing it again*) I don't read.

Adam Oh. I didn't realize. You were never taught to read?

Jacie Why should anyone bother?

Adam Then I'll teach you to read. OK?

Jacie OK.

A soft beeping sound is heard. It seems to emanate from Jacie.

Oh. Oh, dear.

Adam What on earth's that?

Jacie I'm sorry, Adam. I require emptying.

Adam (*alarmed*) Emptying?

Jacie My waste unit appears to have overfilled.

Adam Well, what do you want me to do? How do we stop the noise?

Jacie I need emptying.

Adam (*alarmed*) Do you need to go somewhere and do it? I mean . . .

Jacie I can't do it myself. And it wouldn't be wise for me to move at present. I could spill over . . .

Adam Yes. Right. OK. So, what do you need me to do?

Jacie There is a small trap in my abdomen. You press and twist to open. You ease out the waste bag and then close the trap. It automatically resets.

Adam Right. I'll have to try and do it while no one's watching. Can you keep an eye on that couple?

Jacie Yes.

Adam Are they looking at us now?

Jacie Yes. (*A pause. She waits.*) No. Now.

Adam Right.

He slides under the table and vanishes, hidden by the cloth.
 Unseen by Jacie, under the next, Waiter 1 approaches to take their order. He hesitates.

Jacie Can you find it?

Adam Hang on. It's very fiddly.

Jacie You should be able to feel the button.

Adam Yes. Yes. I've got it.

Jacie That's it. Now, it should push and twist.

Adam Yes, OK. (*struggling*) Come on, come on . . .

Jacie (*wriggling uncomfortably*) Other way!

Adam Sorry. There. Got you.

Jacie Well done!

For the first time she is aware of Waiter 1 standing there. She smiles at him.

82

Adam (*unaware*) All right. Out you come. Out you come. That's it. And – shut you up again. And there we are. (*emerging from under*) One satisfied cust– (*seeing Waiter*) Ah.

Jacie (*smiling at the Waiter*) Do excuse us, it's our anniversary.

Waiter 1 (*frostily*) Ready to order yet, sir?

Adam Not quite.

Waiter 1 Right, sir.

The Waiter moves away.

Jacie He saw you.

Adam Well, he didn't say anything. It's so smart here they're used to that sort of behaviour. I'd better just get rid of this. Won't be a second. (*He walks out of the dining-room past the other table, the bag under his jacket.*)

Girl (*to the Man*) That was so romantic. Why can't you do that sort of thing?

Waiter 1 returns.

Waiter 1 Excuse me, madam.

Jacie Yes?

Waiter 1 Would I be correct in thinking that you're an android, madam?

Jacie (*nervously*) How would you know?

Waiter 1 Because it takes one to know one, madam. (*leaning in to her, softly*) And I want you away from here in twenty seconds or I'll pick you up by the hair and kick you out on your arse personally, you jumped-up little trollop.

Jacie (*smiling, tense*) Does that include service?

Waiter 1 Twenty seconds. And take that pervert with you.

He takes up the menus and moves away. As he does so, Adam comes back clasping a paper.

Jacie Adam, I'm sorry, he –

Adam Come on. Quickly.

Jacie What's the matter?

Adam Our faces are plastered all over the front pages. Look.

Jacie (*rising*) Oh, no.

Adam Come on.

Jacie Where are we going?

Adam Up to the room. I need time to think. I never thought they'd tell the press . . . Walk slowly now. Keep calm. Don't draw attention.

Adam and Jacie walk slowly to the door. Both Waiters watch them.

Jacie (*as she goes*) 'Bye.

On a spur of the moment impulse, she lifts the back of her dress and moons them. Adam remains unaware.
   As this happens, the lights cross fade to:

SCENE SEVEN

The studio.
   Chandler on his own. He is clutching the phone, waiting for news.

Carla enters, pleased.

Carla Relax, we've got them.

Chandler Where?

Carla Would you believe, the Grand Hotel? Calmly eating dinner together in the main dining-room, if you please. We got a tip-off from one of the staff. Lester is going to be so thrilled when he hears about this.

Carla goes. Chandler works his phone.

Chandler (*as he waits*) Come on . . . come on . . . come on . . . (*connecting*) Prim? Listen. They're staying at the Grand . . . Hotel. Yes. But listen, Prim, everyone's on to them . . . You've got to get there before the press find them . . . No 'if's', Prim . . . Well run, then. Run, woman, run, run, run . . . (*He switches off the phone. Clutching his chest*) God! My heart! My heart! I think I'm having a heart attack! No, I'm not. It's just wishful thinking . . .

He disconnects and goes out hurriedly.
As he does so, the lights cross fade to:

SCENE EIGHT

The hotel bedroom.
Adam and Jacie enter.

Adam We'll be safe up here as long as we stay in the room. We'll have to keep out of the public areas till I find us another hotel. Somewhere less conspicuous. Less – particular.

Jacie What's a trollop?

Adam Have they got a phone book in here somewhere? What is a what?

Jacie A trollop?

Adam A trollop? It's an old-fashioned word. It means a whore. A prostitute.

Jacie Oh.

Adam (*still hunting for the phone book*) They must have one somewhere. Why do you ask?

Jacie No reason.

Adam hunts about.

Jacie How do you think the press found out?

Adam How do you think? (*finding the phone book*) Ah!

Jacie Mrs Pepperbloom?

Adam Almost certainly. Now then . . . Hotels? (*He starts to scan the book.*)

Jacie Adam?

Adam Mmm?

Jacie Are we staying the night here?

Adam Yes, just tonight. We should be safe for one night.

Jacie May I try on my things?

Adam What things?

Jacie You know my – new surprise things?

Adam (*distracted*) Yes, sure. Go ahead. Ah. Hotel Mombassa. That sounds a possible.

He starts to dial. Jacie goes into the bathroom.

(*calling to her*) This will only be temporary. Until we can work out something more permanent. I think if I can talk to uncle on my own, I could persuade him to change his mind. If not, I'm going to do a deal with him to rent you for long enough to make the movie elsewhere. There are plenty of other producers, for God's sake. (*into phone*) Hallo. Have you a double room for tomorrow night? . . . No, all night . . . yes . . . that's OK. The name is – Merryweather . . . M – E – R – no, R . . . R for rabbit . . . R . . . could you make that Jones. Yes. Mr and Mrs Jones. All night. Yes. 'Bye. (*calling to Jacie*) Sounds wonderful on the phone.

Adam rises and paces the room as he talks.

Listen, I've been thinking. You really should learn to read, you know. You see, if we do have to go completely independent on this – and I'm prepared to – I'm fully prepared to – then we may have to do it without a great deal of back up, technical back up.

Jacie has re-entered from the bathroom. She is wearing a new nightdress she bought from the shop. She stands posed, waiting for him to see her. He is so engrossed he barely notices.

No programmers. You'll have to work completely hands free. No direct feed at all. Do it the old-fashioned way. Looking at the script, learning it or at least scanning it in advance and then interpreting it entirely for yourself. I know you're capable of that. I have total faith in your talent, Jacie. All we need is a good, supportive director for you. Give you the confidence. Someone who can bring out the best in you. Who you'd feel comfortable working with.

Jacie has gone back into the bathroom again.

If we could get Chance, of course, that would be just wonderful. But there are others, nearly as good. Don't worry – where have you gone? – because all I'm saying is that in the end it's got be your show, Jacie. It's going to

succeed or fail on your personality. I do have some
money. Enough certainly to set this up in a modest way. I
mean, not a fortune but we don't have to go mad. I can
simplify it all down. Reduce the number of locations.
Rent a small studio somewhere.

Jacie returns. She is now wearing a coat.

What I think we – (*noticing her for the first time*) What
are you doing?

Jacie (*grimly*) Nothing. (*She starts to open and shut
drawers.*)

Adam I thought you were getting ready for bed?

Jacie I don't need sleep. I'll just plug into the socket in the
corner there and recharge. I won't bother you. I just make
a faint buzzing.

Adam Don't you want to show me your surprise?

Jacie (*finding a Gideon Bible in one of the drawers*) I
tried it. I looked like a trollop. Here. (*She hands him the
Bible.*)

Adam What's this?

Jacie A book. To read. You can teach me to read. It can
fill in the time.

Adam What's the matter with you?

Jacie Nothing. I want to learn to read, please. Teach me
that book.

Adam This is a Bible.

Jacie I understand that's a very good book.

Adam It's a very long book –

Jacie Please. I want to be right for you. I don't want to spoil your play. Teach me to read. I promise, I'm quick. I learn fast.

Adam Well, all right, if that's what you . . . Come and sit here. I'll show you.

They sit together on the bed side by side. Adam opens the Bible at the beginning.

Right. You understand the general principle of reading? All these different little clumps are words, do you see?

Jacie Yes.

Adam And every word is made up of letters. And there are only twenty-six letters to remember but they make up hundreds of different words. Thousands and thousands of words. Look at this. That is an I, you see. Then that is an N and those two together make the word IN, you see?

Jacie IN . . .

Adam Next word – this is ridiculous –

Jacie The next word . . .?

Adam Next word, T – H – E – that makes THE, you see? So we get IN THE. Now here's a big word B – E – G – that makes BEG or B'G, in this case, because then we get –

Jacie IN

Adam Good.

Jacie IN – IN.

Adam No, ING. That has a G on the end, you see?

Jacie IN THE BEG – INN – ING ... BEGINNING . . .

Adam Good! Then here's a G again which we know, but then here's a new letter O, that's an O and then a D. Those three make GOD.

Jacie GOD. IN THE BEGINNING GOD . . .

Adam Here we go, more new letters. That's a C – then an R – E, we've had before – A, that's an A, then a T. You see that's a T again?

Jacie T.

Adam Then another E there and then D again. And that makes CREATED.

Jacie CREATED.

Adam Then what's this next word?

Jacie THE

Adam Good. CREATED THE –? Now we know these letters – H – that's an H –

Jacie E – A –

Adam Good. New one. V, that's a V – that makes HEAV –?

Jacie EN – HEAVEN.

Adam Good.

Jacie AND THE (*struggling with the word*) Ear – Eart – Ear -tuh – huh

Adam No, that's EARTH.

Jacie IN THE BEGINNING GOD CREATED THE HEAVEN AND THE EARTH –

Adam That is very good. That's impressive.

Jacie (*struggling on*) AND THE EARTH . . .?

Adam W – AS –

Jacie WA – WAS WITH – OUT –

Adam That's an F. A Fuh. Fuh – ORM

Jacie AND THE EARTH WAS WITHOUT FORM AND – (*She hesitates again.*)

Adam VOID. Those two together go OY.

Jacie FORM AND VOID. And DAR –

Adam K, that's a K. DARK – NESS. Those are S's. Like Snakes. Sss.

Jacie NESS – DARKNESS WAS uh –

Adam UPON. That one's a P. Makes a Puh sound.

Jacie . . . UPON THE FACE OF THE DEEP . . . AND THE SPIRIT OF GOD MOVED UPON THE FACE OF THE WATERS –

Adam Very good.

Jacie AND GOD SAID–

Adam L – that's an L. Luh. L – ET

Jacie LET THERE BE – (*She frowns.*)

Adam LIGHT –

Jacie LIGHT . . . AND THERE WAS LIGHT. And there was light. (*She smiles.*) And there was light. How beautiful. I'm longing to know what happens. (*continuing to read rapidly*) And God saw the light, that it was good; and God divided –

Adam Hang on! Hang on! That's enough for one night. (*taking the Bible from her gently*) First things first, please.

> She looks at him. He kisses her gently. She smiles. He smiles at her. Her music starts.

Jacie Do you mind the music? I couldn't help it.

Adam No. It's always good to know how people feel. (*He goes to kiss her again.*)

Jacie (*drawing back momentarily*) Adam, I need to tell you, I am only constructed for simulated sex.

Adam Yes, I gathered that in the restaurant when I was under the . . . I'm sorry, I didn't mean to pry, I just couldn't help noticing.

Jacie They did warn me. Once a man's seen your trap door, he loses all respect for you.

Adam (*smiling*) That's very funny. Where did that come from?

Jacie (*puzzled*) I don't remember.

He kisses her.

Adam, you'll tell me if I'm a trollop, won't you?

Adam I most certainly will. I never kiss trollops on principle.

They kiss again. Jacie's music soars up to a climax as they clasp each other in their arms.
 A sudden heavy knocking on the door.
 The music stops abruptly. They both listen. More knocking.

(*nervously, calling*) Who is it?

Prim (*outside*) Adam, it's Prim. Let me in, quickly.

Adam Prim?

He rushes to the door and opens it. Prim hurries in, still in her nurse's uniform under her coat.

What are you doing here? How on earth did you –?

Prim Quickly. There are press everywhere. The foyer is swarming with them.

Adam Why are they here? What do they want?

Prim Oh, come on. Trainsmith heir in illicit android romance. The story of the decade. I don't know how we get you out of here. They're sure to have the back doors covered, they're not that stupid.

Adam How did you find us?

Prim (*producing a small gadget from her pocket*) Your beloved gives off a coded signal every fifteen minutes, didn't you know? Now, if they're smart, they'll start working down the names of the guests one by one. They'll get to you eventually. What name did you book in under?

Adam Hornblower.

Prim I'm amazed they're not banging on the door already. Excuse the strange dress. I was about to have to make a cringingly embarrassing appearance as Nurse Bridget. (*to Jacie*) Thanks to you.

Jacie Oh.

Adam Wait a minute. They're looking for me and a nurse, aren't they? They're still expecting a nurse? Right?

Prim Yes, but – (*comprehending*) Oh no, you . . . No. I couldn't.

Adam Just long enough for Jacie to get clear. Please.

Prim Why are you doing this, Adam? After all I said to you. All my warnings.

Adam Please, Prim.

Prim (*resignedly*) Oh, well. It's only jail, isn't it? (*She goes to check the corridor.*)

Adam Jacie, pack your things. Prim and I are going to draw them round to the main foyer. As soon as the coast is clear, go down the escape stairs at the end of the passage there and out of the back door. Yes?

Jacie Yes.

Adam (*fumbling in his pocket*) Hail a taxi, I'll give you some money, and ask to go to the Hotel Mombassa. It's 54 Kenway Street, can you remember that? (*handing her some cash*) Here. Tell them you are Mrs Jones, that you want your room a day early and your husband will be along shortly. All right? Do not tell them how you were once mauled in a big game hunt or fell out of a hot air balloon. Don't say anything else. Stay put and wait for me. Can you do that?

Jacie Yes.

Adam Then off you go. Get your things together.

Jacie obediently heads towards the bathroom.

(*as she goes*) Jacie.

Jacie Yes?

Adam I love you.

Jacie Oh.

She goes off into the bathroom. Prim returns.

Adam All clear out there?

Prim All clear.

Adam Ready to face them, then?

Prim I suppose so. (*as they go*) Now I'm a nurse who sleeps in hotels with strange men. God, this will make my mother so happy . . .

Adam Come on, then.

Adam and Prim leave. As they do so, the lights cross fade to:

SCENE NINE

A sleazy hotel room. Distant music and occasional voices.
Jacie lets herself in and switches on the light. It makes little difference. She stands and surveys the space. She examines the bed cautiously. She unpacks her carrier, taking her dress and new shoes and putting them carefully on a chair. She sits on the bed.
She seems quite disoriented and emits rather tense music.

Jacie Jacie. I – love – you. Love – you – Jacie. Love? (*slowly losing control, increasingly rapidly*) Oh, my sweet love, why are you throwing back my love – my love will last a thousand – love is blind – loves a lover – love's triangle – let your love surround me, loving you – love me do – loved one, lovesick, love seat, love song, lovelock, lovelorn, love lies, love dies, love bites, love leaves, love leaves you bleeding, love that leads you on and lets you – let me love you – lie me in your arms and love me – lull me – lose me – love me – love me – let me hear you whisper loving love, my lover, lay me, lay me, love, oh lovely, lovely, lovely, lovely, YES, my darling love . . . (*She stops abruptly. After a pause*) Oh, lord love a duck.

In a second, the door bursts open and a mini-skirted, heavily made-up woman enters.

Prostitute (*seeing Jacie*) Oh, sorry, dear.

Jacie The door doesn't lock.

Prostitute Just as well in this place, isn't it? Don't want to get locked in here, do you? I was told this room was free. I've got a double booking and I need the space. You going to be in here for long?

Jacie Er . . . about two or three days, I think . . .

Prostitute Two or three days? Who've you got, a male voice choir?

Jacie No. Just my – husband . . .

Prostitute Your *husband*?

Jacie Mr Jones. I'm Mrs Jones. We're both staying here.

Prostitute Staying here?

Jacie Yes.

Prostitute You're not working for Turkey?

Jacie Turkey?

Prostitute The owner, dear.

Jacie No. I work for Tri-Lab.

Prostitute Tri-Lab? Come off it. No one in their right mind would stay here through choice. Mrs Jones! Who you working for? Who's working you, darling?

Jacie No one's working me. I'm free. I'm working myself.

Prostitute Well, you'd better not be found here, dear. This is Turkey's pitch and he doesn't love freebodies, not at all he doesn't.

Jacie I am not a trollop.

Prostitute You're not a what?

Jacie A trollop. I am not a whore. I'm not paid. Nobody pays me.

Prostitute Oh? A real lady, are you? I see. Nice coat. Where d'you get it?

Jacie It was a present.

Prostitute Lovely. So was this, actually. Who paid for those shoes, then? And that dress? Bet that cost a bit.

96

Someone's been a bit grateful, haven't they? Then I suppose if it's not cash that makes it smart, doesn't it? Listen, it's none of my business if you want to sless yourself but if he's a man and he's brought you here, he's working you, sweetheart. No two ways. Because that's all they want us for. And if he's spinning you something other, then he's lying his little thieving heart out. Because as soon as he's taken what he wants from you he'll be scarped. So if you're clinging to that, then all I can say is you're in for a deal of deject, and if you'll take my premon you'll get the stripe out of here now, before Turkey catches you.

Jacie (*angrily*) Look, you just stump in your own cradle, sis, and stop trying to molly me cause I fend me own square, right? You just piss back to your slam and don't start giving me no worldlies because I done more scrape than you've had hot takers so why don't you just go scrub your charmers, eh?

Prostitute (*digesting this, rather stunned*) You're in trouble you are, darling. Real trouble. Turkey'll deal with you. (*She goes out.*)

Jacie stands for a second. She is very miserable. Suddenly, she gives an involuntary sob. Then another. They convulse her body and appear to take her by surprise. She recovers as suddenly as she started. She removes her coat. She is still wearing her nightdress underneath. She takes her Gideon Bible from her carrier and starts reading.

Jacie 'Unto the woman he said: I will greatly multiply thy sorrow and thy conception: in sorrow thou shalt bring forth children: and thy desire shall be to thy husband, and he shall rule over thee.' Oh.

She shuts the book hurriedly. She takes out her nurse's uniform and with difficulty, puts it on. She gathers up

*the rest of her belongings, dress, shoes, Bible, coat and
stuffs them into her carrier. She makes as if to leave,
hears someone coming, and instead sits miserably
hunched in a corner. Adam enters.*

Adam Jacie! Thank heavens. I've been in and out of a
dozen rooms looking for you. What a place! I've learnt
more in ten minutes here than I – Jacie, what are you
doing? Why have you put all that on?

Silence.

Are you all right? (*studying her*) Have you been crying?

Jacie pulls away.

Is it this place? We won't be here for long, I promise. (*He
waits.*) Jacie?

Jacie What do you want, Adam? From me. I don't know
what you want.

Adam You. I want you.

Jacie What for?

Adam What?

Jacie What do you want me for?

Adam I don't understand your question. I want you – for
you.

Jacie To be in your programme?

Adam Partly – yes. That was the initial reason, I admit.
But – not any more.

Jacie If we had no programme. If there was never a
chance of doing what you've written – would you still
want me?

Adam Of course.

Jacie What for?

Adam I've told you. Because I love you. I love you, Jacie.

Jacie I am not Jacie, Adam. I am JCF 31 triple 3. There is no Jacie. There's no real me. I'm a machine, Adam. I wasn't taught to think of myself as that, but I acknowledge now that I am. On the one hand, it's a fact that every day we stay together, you'll change and I'll stay the same. I'm nineteen years old and I have been like this since the day I was made.

Adam (*smiling*) Well, I'd think of that as an advantage. You'll save yourself a fortune in beauty treatments and –

Jacie Adam, you must listen. Don't laugh at me. I'm trying to say something and it's difficult for me.

Adam I'm sorry. Go on.

Jacie But on the other hand, despite that, I will only ever be what people want me to be. I'll be a nurse or a soldier or a runaway bride or grumpy woman in tea shop. But I can never be me. So I can't do what you want me to. You're asking too much of me, Adam. Yes, I can *play* your Jacie. I can play her just as you want her to be. I'm good at that. That's what I was made for. But I can never *be* your Jacie. Do you see the difference? I've been miscast, you see. Please. Take me back. Audition failed. Leave your name at the door. We'll keep in touch.

Adam Oh, come on, you don't mean that –

Jacie (*increasingly agitated*) I want to go back, I want to melt down. I don't want to be like this any more. It's too painful. Nothing's working. I can't control me. Look at me, I'm crying and I have no stimulus to cry. I'm so unhappy, Adam. You don't know how I feel . . .

Adam I do, Jacie. I know . . .

Jacie You can't know! If you knew and if you loved me, you wouldn't let this happen to me.

Adam Listen, once we're out of here, we'll –

Jacie What? Get married? Have children? Become sheep farmers?

Adam (*angered*) Where is all this coming from? What programme are you in now, for God's sake?

Jacie (*in a quite uncontrolled fury*) This is not a programme. This is me talking, Adam. And I'm lost and I don't know what I'm doing and nobody's telling me and the only person in the world that I trust is standing there talking to me like a child. And I refuse to be treated like that, do you hear me? You make plans for our future without consulting me, you dress me up like some mindless puppet, you humiliate me in shops and restaurants, move me in and out of hotel rooms and make me feel like a second-hand trollop and then you won't even make an effort to understand what I'm trying to tell you – well, you can just go to hell and screw yourself and see if I care, you – stupid fuck dyke!

Silence. Jacie stands breathless from her outburst.

Was that me?

Adam (*smiling at her*) It's certainly nothing I ever wrote.

Jacie Oh, God.

Adam Jacie . . . Sit down. (*Pause.*) You need to sit down. Please . . .

Jacie sits.

I love you, Jacie. I really do. I've not had a great deal of experience in these matters but I think what you're trying to tell me, in a roundabout sort of way, is that you love me too.

Jacie Am I?

Another silence.

Oh, Adam. I can't cope with this. I really can't.

The door bursts open and Turkey, a pimp and owner of the hotel bursts in.

Turkey All right! (*pointing at Jacie*) You! Out, now.

Jacie What?

Turkey Go on. Get your arse out of here, you.

Adam Now, just a minute –

Turkey (*to Adam*) Keep out the way, mate. No quarrel with you. Just the tart. (*to Jacie, raising his hand*) Come on, unless you want to feel it. Come on!

Jacie Get out of here.

Turkey What?

Jacie I said get out. Don't you realize I am trying to have the first serious conversation I have ever had in my life and I refuse to be interrupted by you, you third-rate pimp!

Adam Jacie!

Turkey What did you say to me?

Jacie You heard. Leave us alone.

Suddenly there is a knife in Turkey's hand.

Turkey You're just about due for surgery, aren't you? Learn a few manners.

Jacie faces him. Turkey lunges at her. She steps back.

Adam No!

Jacie (*calmly*) It's all right, Adam . . .

Adam No . . .

Jacie He won't hurt me.

Turkey (*lunging in at Jacie*) We'll have a try, won't we?

Adam Jacie!

He leaps between them to protect Jacie. He fails to deflect the knife and is stabbed in the side.

Jacie Adam!

Adam collapses on the bed.

Turkey That was stupid. That was so stupid . . .

Jacie (*advancing on Turkey , fiercely*) Right! Drop the knife!

Turkey Eh? What is this?

Jacie I said drop the knife, punk.

Turkey lunges again. Jacie reacts like lightning, gripping his wrist. Turkey drops the knife. Jacie turns him round, plants her knee in his back and forces him to the floor.

Jacie (*bringing his other arm behind him*) Special vice unit. You are well and truly nicked, mister!

She instinctively gropes at her belt for her handcuffs but can't find any. She yanks Turkey to his feet.

Turkey Aaah! Easy! Easy!

Jacie (*threateningly in his ear*) And if I see you in here again, you'll be talking out of some alternative orifice, all right? You listening to me, sunshine?

Turkey Yes.

Jacie Then get out!

She gives him a fierce shove and Turkey hurtles out of the door. There is a crash and a groan. Jacie turns immediately to Adam.

Adam?

Adam groans. Jacie hurries to tend to him.

Adam? Please be all right. (*removing his jacket*) Oh. (*She surveys the blood on his shirt.*) Oh no, oh no, oh no. Adam?

Adam (*weakly*) It's all right. It's worse than it looks . . .

Jacie Is it?

Adam I mean, it's not as worse as it's – aaahh! – it's OK.

Jacie You need a doctor.

Adam No, no. I just need you, Jacie.

Jacie Adam, you're bleeding very badly.

Adam You were wonderful. Where did that one come from?

Jacie (*as she tends to him*) *Phantom Squad*. It was a pilot for a series they never made. I played Terry. A closet lesbian. She was blown up by terrorists. It looks very deep, Adam.

Adam Just hold me. You see you can't leave me, Jacie. To hell with looking after you. I need you to look after me, don't you see? I need you, Jacie.

Jacie (*rocking him, gently*) Oh, Adam. Please don't die. I'm the one that always dies. You mustn't die, Adam . . . You've been my partner since the start.

Sad, end-of-the-movie music comes from her.

Ever since we were rookie kids together at the academy.

You've saved my life so many times, I've lost count. Like the occasion on the top of that burning building, do you remember? When I was –

Adam Jacie . . .

Jacie Mmm?

Adam Would you just shut up and let me die . . .

Jacie (*gently*) Sure thing, partner . . .

> *Music ends. Adam is asleep. The music stops. She slips him from her lap and gently lowers him on to the bed. She picks up his jacket and takes some money from the pocket. She returns the jacket, looks at Adam, kisses him softly on the forehead and tiptoes out.*
> *As she does so, the lights cross fade to:*

SCENE TEN

The studio.
> *Lester is wheeled in by Marmion. Carla follows excitedly.*

Marmion . . . But if the android's returned, then where's my nephew?

Carla He's in hospital, Lester. There was some sort of fight. It's not very clear. Apparently, Adam was stabbed. Don't be alarmed, not too seriously but enough to –

Marmion Where? Where was he stabbed?

Carla Just to the side of his rib cage, about two inches below –

Marmion No, I meant where was he stabbed? What location?

Carla Oh, I see. In some terrible hotel – virtually a brothel . . .

Jacie enters. Behind her come Chandler, Prim and Trudi.

Marmion What the hell's an android doing in a brothel?

Carla Here it is. You can ask it yourself.

Marmion Which of you was responsible for bringing it back?

Trudi It came back of its own accord, Mr Trainsmith.

Marmion Its own accord? Does it have a homing beacon?

Prim I think you should ask Jacie, Mr Trainsmith.

Marmion It's not Mr Trainsmith's custom to speak to androids.

Prim Yes, but if you listen to her, you might –

Carla (*sharply*) You heard what he said. Mr Trainsmith does not talk to androids. Personally, I think the sooner that thing is melted down the better. It has involved Mr Trainsmith in a close personal scandal. It has also made this corporation a near laughing stock and has endangered the life of a human being which is in total conflict with the first directive –

Marmion Mrs Pepperbloom! One moment, please!

Prim I think you should talk to her, Mr Trainsmith, I really do.

After a second, Lester comes to a decision. Marmion turns him to face Jacie.

Marmion Now you listen to me – (*to the others*) – what name do you call it?

Prim Jacie.

Marmion Listen to me, Jacie. Do you know who I am?

Jacie Yes, Mr Trainsmith.

Marmion Can you tell me how my nephew came to be injured?

Jacie He was trying to – protect me . . .

Marmion To protect you?

Jacie Yes. He did it for me. He thought I was in danger.

Carla Oh, I don't think we need to waste any more time on this regurgitated romantic drivel. The sooner the thing's melted down, the sooner –

Marmion One moment. You say he thought you were in danger. What danger were you in? It would take a thermal missile to damage you . . .

Jacie It was – instinctive.

Chandler (*muttering*) This is all my fault.

Prim No. It's my fault. If I'd only traced –

Jacie (*vehemently*) It was *my* fault. This is my fault.

Carla Oh, this is quite obscene. The thing's trying to make out Adam was in love with it . . .

Marmion I'm well aware of what it's trying to make out, Carla – (*to Jacie*) And what made you come back here?

Jacie I – (*She hesitates.*)

Marmion Did Adam send you back?

Jacie No. He doesn't know I'm here.

Marmion Then tell me why you came back.

Jacie I was not right. Not right.

Carla Well, at least it acknowledges the source of the blame which is something to commend it, I suppose.

Marmion I am wholly in agreement with that sentiment, Mrs Pepperbloom.

Carla (*rather smugly*) Thank you, Lester.

Marmion I only wish that other employees could be quite so objective about themselves. You see, what I particularly regret about this whole business, which since no one was badly injured can only be seen as a squall in a domestic teacup –

Carla Hardly that –

Marmion What I particularly regret is that someone within this corporation chose deliberately to leak things to the press –

Carla Yes, that was all very –

Marmion And I was particularly sad to learn that the leak came from you, Mrs Pepperbloom.

Carla That is totally untrue, Lester. I don't know who told you –

Marmion It's one thing to go behind my back and leak embarrassing, potentially damaging information to the press, it is quite another to be caught doing it.

Carla You can't possibly prove all this.

Marmion If you don't want to get caught, Mrs Pepperbloom, may I suggest in future you don't make anonymous calls to newspapers that I happen to own from phones in offices that I also happen to own.

Carla I really can't believe in all seriousness that you're accusing me –

Marmion In all seriousness, Mrs Pepperbloom. There is a third, far more important reason why I'm going to have you removed from your post –

Carla (*weakly*) You're going to what?

Marmion Do you know what the motto of this company is, Mrs Pepperbloom? Do you recall it, at all? I'm sure you do. It's on our notepaper, it's on every office wall. It is in letters of gold inscribed on our boardroom wall in Seattle. Two words, Mrs Pepperbloom. Nothing – Personal. Meaning the company is bigger than the individual. Nothing can be allowed to get personal. Nothing. Not for board members, not for vice presidents, not for senior executives, not for the individual rank and file on the floor here and particularly not for the goddamned artists. You chose to get personal, Mrs Pepperbloom, and not only that, not just with a person but personal with an actoid. I am dismissing you not just for disloyalty, Carla, but for sheer, downright stupidity.

Carla (*speechless*) I can't believe . . . you can't . . . I mean, this is absolutely . . . I expect my pension rights to be honoured . . . (*to the others*) Aren't any of you going to say anything on my behalf? Cowards! No, what can you expect from a bunch of second-rate, talentless, inadequate lorn bosers!

Jacie stifles a laugh.

(*turning to vent her fury on her*) Well, at least I'll have the satisfaction of knowing that you're not going to be around much longer. The sooner you're melted down the better for everyone, you jumped-up, poisonous little actoid.

Jacie (*smiling*) Thank you, Mrs Pepperbloom. I'm sure that's nothing personal.

Lester emits another of his rusty laughs.

Carla (*raising her hand to slap her*) Why, you insolent –

Carla goes to make the blow but Jacie's instincts are far too swift. She catches Carla's wrist and holds it for a second, inches from her face.

You see this? Now it's attacking me. It's attacking me.

Trudi Carla, if that blow had landed, you'd have broken every bone in your hand.

A slight pause. Jacie releases Carla's wrist. Carla goes out, without another word.

Chandler I suppose some good always comes out of something.

Jacie Excuse me.

Jacie starts to walk away. Suddenly, unexpectedly, we hear Lester's voice.

Lester Jacie.

Jacie turns, like everyone, quite startled by this.

Come back here a minute.

Marmion (*echoing him*) Come back here a minute.

Jacie does so obediently.

Lester Closer.

Marmion Closer.

Jacie moves closer to Lester.

She's an actoid, Mr Trainsmith. Do be careful.

Lester Oh, do shut up, Marmion.

Marmion Shut up, Marmion.

Lester (*fiercely*) Look, just go away, man.

Marmion Er – oh, yes, Mr Trainsmith.

Marmion unplugs himself and leaves.

Lester You see, I can use my voice if I need to. It's just often more convenient to say unpalatable things through a third party. And I seem to spend most of my life these days saying unpalatable things. It also means I don't waste time on small talk. Now listen to me. Are you listening?

Jacie Yes.

Lester I have a proposal to make. I've seen your work. I've seen the impression you've made on the people around you. You've made friends. You've even inspired a sort of cock-eyed loyalty, particularly from my nephew. And I'm also impressed at the way you came back here today. Even for an actoid, that took a lot of courage.

Jacie I had to. If I hadn't –

Lester (*gently*) Please, let me finish. I'll tell you something. At one time I never liked you things. Quite frankly, I never really trust any machinery and I mistrust artificial intelligence even more. I'm an old Luddite at heart, if you know what I mean by that. Which is ironic when you consider I run the largest company in the world, dedicated exclusively to the production and development of artificial intelligence. But now I'm getting older – incredibly older – and I'm becoming increasingly reliant on artificial intelligence. By the time I'm a hundred and twenty – which my doctors confidently assure me I shall reach – I shall probably look a little like you. Which wouldn't be at all a bad thing. Anyway. Here's the proposition. I have just had to part company, as you know, with Mrs Pepperbloom in order for her to further her career. I would like to offer you her job as Regional Director. What do you say to that?

Trudi He's gone crazy . . .

Chandler Completely gone . . . completely . . .

Prim Maybe.

Lester I think it's time we gave artificial intelligence a trial canter, don't you? You seem as good a risk as any. Though I warn you, if you mess things up, then I will melt you down personally. What do you say?

A silence.

Jacie I'm not right.

Lester You'd get training. You'd have an assistant. Loads of assistants.

Jacie No, you don't understand. I'm not right. I was not right for Adam.

Lester Then what do you suggest we do to put you right?

Jacie Like she said, I should be melted down.

Chandler Oh, come on, Jacie . . .

Prim Jacie!

Jacie I'm unstable. I no longer control my feelings.

Prim (*looking at Chandler*) If that was a criterion we'd all be melted down.

Lester Is that seriously what you want?

Jacie I think it's what should happen.

Lester But is it what you truly want?

Jacie (*distressed*) I don't know what I truly want. (*more softly*) Please!

Lester If that's your final decision. I think it's wrong and I'm a little sad. I think you're rather special. You made me laugh. On two occasions. Which is twice more than my three wives ever managed. (*to Trudi*) Would you mind calling Marmion, young lady? I think I've done enough talking for one day. He's probably sulking somewhere out there.

Trudi goes out.

Prim (*tearfully*) We can't let this happen to her.

Lester Oh, come now. Don't get sentimental. If you support greater freedom for them, you have to start by respecting their decisions.

Prim (*upset*) I think it's just terrible, I really do. We'd all grown so fond of her.

She hurries out, passing Marmion.

Lester Ah, Marmion. Good. Jacie, I'm asking Marmion to leave my private number on the desk here. If you change your mind within the next hour, you can call me. I shall be en route to Rome.

Marmion Rangoon, Mr Trainsmith. (*He places a card on the console.*)

Lester Rangoon, Rio, Rome. They're all the same to someone in my condition. Plug in then, Marmion, plug in and take over.

Marmion Yes, Mr Trainsmith. (*as he wheels Lester out*) This'll be the first time I've been turned down by an android. Think it over, Jacie. Goodbye!

Lester is wheeled out by Marmion.
Silence.

Chandler You realize what you've done? The classic

Oliver Hardy. You've just slammed a door in your own face. And not just in your own. In every single android face.

Jacie is silent.

Don't you think you owe it to them to accept?

Jacie still doesn't reply.

No, you're probably right, why should you? Trainsmith's only offered you the job so's he'll look enlightened. The rest of us know he's doing it to try and break the union but it'll all be done in the name of progress so who'll notice? You're quite right. Why help him? But what about Adam? Don't you think you owe him something? Doesn't it worry you that he loves you?

Jacie He doesn't love me.

Chandler He apparently risked his life for you. When you weren't even in any real danger. That makes him either in love or an idiot.

Jacie It was just instinctive. (*Pause.*) All right. Maybe he does love me. All the more reason I should melt down. Do you think I could bear it if anything like that ever happened to him again? Just because he loves me? It's terrifying.

Chandler But don't you think that the only reason you're terrified at the thought that something might happen to him again because he loves you, is because you care too much about him to want to see anything happen to him? Or to put it slightly more simply, because you love him?

Jacie tries to sort out this complex logic for a second, then gives up.

Jacie (*with a wail*) I don't know.

113

Chandler (*yelling at her*) You don't know? What kind of machine are you, for God's sake? I thought you were supposed to be logical.

Jacie (*in tears again*) Well, I'm not any more, am I? I'm a mess!

Chandler You certainly are. You're stupid as well! My mother's food mixer had more sense than you have.

A silence.

Jacie Why me? Why choose me? You said yourself, there's thousands of us, all alike, what's so special about me? Am I so unique?

Chandler Unique? Now that is a grossly misused word, particularly in this business. No, Jacie, you are not unique. No one's unique. On any project, the most you can hope for creatively is to be conveniently essential to it. But forget unique. The road to stardom is strewn with the forgotten bodies of people who were told – usually by some stupid critic – and, worse still, *believed*, they were unique. You have any doubt, you're looking at one.

Jacie Then why do you still bother?

Chandler Because I still believe I have it in me to create something unique. (*smiling at her bewilderment*) I'm sorry, Jacie. Don't even try to understand that.

Jacie shakes her head. A Technician appears in the doorway. He has a handful of straps and restraints.

Technician (*aware he's interrupted something*) Er – excuse me. Is there an actoid here for the factory?

Jacie Yes. Me.

Technician Oh. Right.

Chandler You won't need all that stuff. She doesn't need restraining. This one's volunteering.

Technician Volunteering?

Chandler I think she's researching for Mary Queen of Scots. Or Mary's little lamb or something.

The Technician takes Jacie by the arm.

You don't need to do this. You're going way over the top again, you know that?

Jacie It won't matter much soon, will it?

Technician Coming then?

Jacie I'm coming.

On her way to the door, she contrives to do a comedy trip.

Whoops! Leave 'em laughing, folks!

Jacie and the Technician leave.
Chandler is left on his own.

Chandler Who's been teaching her *that*? Completely mistimed. If you're going to use a comedy trip, if you insist on using it, you've got to make sure you're not already drawing attention to your feet, otherwise the audience is expecting it. (*yelling after her*) I've told you time after time comedy is *surprise*, otherwise . . . it's . . . Oh, to hell with her. Why do they all want to play Hamlet? Or Hedda? (*He opens a drawer and produces the bottle of Scotch and swigs from it.*) Such a waste! All that potential! Who cares if it's an actoid or a person or a performing parrot? If it makes you laugh, treasure it. Tragedy? You can get that in the street being run over.

Adam enters. He walks stiffly. His side is bandaged under his shirt.

Ah! The author returns. Perfect timing. My life's just run out of script.

Adam I saw a lorry driving out, was that Uncle Lester or . . .?

Chandler That was Jacie. In a box.

Adam (*alarmed*) Jacie? Oh, my God. No!

Chandler That's what she wanted, Adam.

Adam No!

Chandler We tried to reason with her. But it has to be said she's an extraordinarily unreasonable actoid. Trainsmith even offered her a job. Mrs Pepperbloom's job. Would you believe he fired Carla?

Adam Then why didn't Jacie . . .? Why on earth didn't she . . .?

Chandler She was only a poor machine. You screwed her up, Adam. It was your fault entirely. Poor thing didn't know whether she was coming or going. Just another sad victim of cupid's custard pie. Now she's gone to a better place, to make her final pratfall in the sky. Breaking the habit of a lifetime, would you care to join me for a drink?

Adam shakes his head.

Be warned, I will never ask you again. See you around.

He goes out.
    Adam is now on his own.
    He sits at the console, very unhappy.

Adam Why? Why? Why, Jacie?

Despairingly, he jabs at the console. He succeeds in animating the actoids. The Farmer and his Wife appear and restart part of their earlier sequence, only this time without Jacie.

116

Farmer (*calling*) Mother . . . Mother . . . Quickly! Give me a hand here.

Adam Oh, no . . . (*He stabs vainly at the console to stop it, then gives up.*)

Wife (*rushing to help*) What is it, Father? What's happened?

Farmer I don't know for certain. I found her lying by the side of the road. It may have been a hit and run. Come on, get her on to the bed.

Struggling, they mime getting Jacie to the bed and laying her down.

There! That's it!

Wife She doesn't look right.

Farmer She's not right. We may need to fetch the doctor.

Wife He's twenty mile away. He'll never get through in this snow.

Farmer Aye, true. Three metres deep it is up at Hegg's Bottom.

Wife (*to Jacie*) Are you all right, love? Can you hear me? Oh, she's that cold, poor little thing. I'll get her a rug, Father . . . What's she saying? (*to Jacie*) Are you trying to tell us something, love?

Under this, Jacie re-enters unseen by Adam. She is rather dusty and unkempt.

What's she trying to say, Father?

Farmer If you shut up a minute, Mother, we might be able to hear her.

They lean closer to the bed to hear.

Come on, lass, what are you trying to say?

Adam is aware of someone. He turns and sees Jacie. He stares at her incredulously.

Jacie I – fell – off – the lorry . . .

The Farmer and his Wife remain frozen. Adam rises. A moment.

Adam Jacie?

Romantic music from Jacie as they move together.

Jacie I couldn't go through with it. Chandler was right. I think I must be in love.

Adam (*kissing her*) You sound that way to me.

Jacie Oh, Adam. I'm so happy.

Adam (*smiling*) By the way. Congratulations, Regional Director. Wonderful.

Jacie (*running her fingers through his hair*) Yes, that reminds me, I'd better make that call to Lester. (*She goes and retrieves Lester's card.*)

Adam (*suddenly anxious*) This won't change things, will it? I mean, even if you accept this job, you won't give up acting? You can still do my show?

Jacie (*hesitating*) Probably. (*She picks up the phone.*)

Adam Jacie, there's no question of probably. It has to be you. You're – unique. I'll fetch the others. This is a celebration. We are actually going to make our programme. The full two-hour special, eh? A whole two hours.

Jacie I think probably seventy-five minutes, darling.

Adam What? (*uncertainly*) Yes. Well. We'll talk about it, won't we? Sure. Won't be a minute.

He goes out. Jacie puts the card into the phone and waits for it to dial. She looks around her and at the still frozen actoids in mid-scene.

Jacie (*softly*) All right, people, let's go to work. (*incisively*) Action!

As she speaks into the phone, the music surges and the other actoids obediently restart their scene.
Curtain.